FOOTPRINTS OF JESUS

Part 1

Footprints of Jesus

PART I
FROM MANGER TO MANHOOD

By W. L. Emmerson

Author of "Bible Certainties," "The Bible Speaks,"
"God's Good News," etc.

ILLUSTRATED WITH MASTERPIECES OF
SACRED ART AND SCENES FROM
THE HOLY LAND

THE STANBOROUGH PRESS LTD., WATFORD, HERTS.

CONTENTS

ACKNOWLEDGMENTS

OUR grateful acknowledgments are due to the following for permission to reproduce their copyright pictures: BRAUN ET CIE, p. 155; CAMERA CLIX, pp. 16 20 24 27 28 48 60 64 76 84 88 96 112 116 143 172 180; JOHN H. EGGERS and the BROOKLYN MUSEUM, pp. 80 92 120 128 136 144 152 156 160 164; EYRE & SPOTTISWOODE, pp. 62 150; W. E. FILMER, pp. 125 140 184 185; HANFSTAENGL, pp. 8 36 104 107 132 176; S. H. HORN, p. 140; A. R. MOWBRAY & CO., p. 46; T. NELSON & SONS, p. 56; PALESTINE EXPLORATION FUND, rear endsheet; RELIGIOUS NEWS SERVICE, pp. 118 170; STUDIO LISA, pp. 31 47 143 163; THREE LIONS, pp. 32 40 44 45 72 100 101 111 124 141 front endsheet; C. D. WATSON, pp. 101 168 169 185.

Illustrations

BIBLE PICTURES (In Colour)

SCENES IN BIBLE LANDS (In Colour)

MONOCHROME ILLUSTRATIONS

First Tidings of the Saviour

IN a little glen among the hills of Judah, about five miles west of the city of Jerusalem, nestles a tiny village. What it was called in the days of Jesus we do not know, but today, it goes by the name of Ain Karem. Its little flat-topped houses climb either side of the valley, while among and round about the dwellings are fruit orchards, olive groves, and vineyards. Several little springs provide water for the community, and through the village a steep road runs up and over the ridge in the direction of the capital.

Here, it is believed, in the days of Herod the Great, vassal "King of the Jews" under the Roman Cæsar, lived an aged priest, Zacharias, and his wife Elisabeth. They were a godly pair, diligently keeping the commandments of the Lord, and faithful in all the observances of synagogue and temple.

Zacharias belonged to the course of Abia, the eighth of the twenty-four groups of priests organized by David to carry on the services of the temple. Twice a year since he came to manhood he had gone up that road to Jerusalem to carry out his seven days of ministry in the temple, and now his turn had come again. He gathered together the clean linen garments of his office and his linen turban, bade good-bye to Elisabeth, and set off up the hill road for the holy city.

Entering by a gate on the west side, he skirted the great towers of the palace of Herod which dominated the west wall of the city and made his way through the jostling crowds down the street leading to the temple area. Crossing the great bridge that spanned the Cheesemongers' Valley between the two horseshoe-like hills on which Jerusalem was built, he entered the temple enclosure and soon reached the quarters where the ministering priests lived during their time of service.

Each morning of the ensuing week he rose before dawn, put on his ceremonial

The angel Gabriel announces to Zacharias that he is to be the father of the forerunner of Christ.

13

garments, and went out to join the company of priests on duty. Assembling in the Hall of Hewn Stones in the Priests' Court they cast lots for the various tasks, the most coveted of which was the offering of incense upon the golden altar in the holy place. As there were thousands of priests who carried out their rotas of service in the temple during the year, this special privilege was not likely to come to anyone more than once in a lifetime, if at all, and such a one was called "rich" for ever after. Great, therefore, was the joy of Zacharias when the lot one morning fell on him. It may have been for the morning sacrifice or for the evening, as two priests each day were given this sacred office.

As soon as the sacrifice had been prepared on the great altar, Zacharias advanced with two assistants up the marble steps and through the massive door into the sanctuary court. Drawing aside the beautiful purple veil before the holy place, they passed into the first apartment.

To the left of them as they entered was the seven-branched golden candlestick, its lamps newly trimmed by one of their fellow priests, and on the right the table of showbread with the twelve cakes of bread upon it. Directly in front of them, before the veil separating the holy place from the holy of holies, which only the high priest might enter, was the beautiful gold-plated altar of incense.

One of Zacharias' assistants went forward and removed the dead embers of the previous offering and retired. The other then moved to the altar and spread upon it coals from the altar of burnt offering. When he too had retired, Zacharias was left alone in the holy apartment. Reverently he stepped forward and spread incense from the golden censer he carried upon the altar. As it kindled, the chamber was filled with a fragrant perfume.

After a prayer for the blessing of God upon Israel he was about to leave to give the benediction to the crowd of worshippers assembled in the outer court, when he was suddenly conscious of an angelic form standing between the altar and the table of showbread. At first he was transfixed by fear at the heavenly visitation, but his fears were quickly allayed by the angel's greeting, "Fear not, Zacharias: for thy prayer is heard; and thy wife Elisabeth shall bear thee a son."

Zacharias could not believe his ears. He had been anticipating the joy of telling Elisabeth how the lot to minister at the altar of incense had fallen on him, but this was undreamed-of news. It had always been their greatest sorrow that no child had been born into their home, and now after all these years of waiting, his wife was to have a child.

But the angel had something even more momentous to tell him. Their child, he said, would do more than bring joy and gladness to them in their old age. He would be born for special service for God. "He shall be great in the sight of the Lord," declared the angel, and his name was to be Johanan or John, which significantly meant, "Jehovah will be gracious."

Zacharias and Elisabeth were to bring up their child in austere simplicity and carefully shelter him from the worldly pleasures of his day. Upon him was to descend the "spirit and power" of the great prophet Elijah, and he would go forth "to make ready a people prepared for the Lord."

All through the centuries of Israel's history the faithful people of God had waited for the appearance of the Messiah, their Deliverer. For nearly six centuries the land and people of Israel had been trodden under foot by one conqueror after another, Assyrian, Babylonian, Persian, Greek, and now they were enduring the Roman occupation, the most grievous of all. In the hearts of priests and people was an ardent longing for the promised deliverance. To be sure, the great majority thought only of physical relief and national liberation, but there were those who longed even more for spiritual deliverance from the bondage of sin and for the coming of the reign of righteousness upon the earth. Now Zacharias learned that the coming of Messiah was at hand, and that his promised son was actually to herald His advent!

Like his ancestor Abraham before him, Zacharias responded incredulously, "Whereby shall I know this? I am an old man, and my wife well stricken in years."

To his amazed ears the angel went on: "I am Gabriel, that stand in the presence of God; and am sent to speak unto thee, and to show thee these glad tidings." His angelic visitor was none other than the one who had communicated to Daniel the wonderful prophecies concerning the Messiah; and now God had sent him to announce to Zacharias their imminent fulfilment. Surely he could ask no more authoritative assurance than that!

But Zacharias had asked for a sign and a sign should be given him, one which would, at the same time, be a judgment upon his unbelief.

"Behold, thou shalt be dumb, and not able to speak, until the day that these things shall be performed," Gabriel declared, and with these words he vanished.

The interview with the angel had considerably extended the time Zacharias had spent in the holy place, and the waiting people were beginning to wonder what had happened. No priest would stay longer than was necessary in the awesome presence of God in the inner sanctuary. But just as one of the priests was about to enter to see what had befallen the old man, the curtain was drawn aside and Zacharias emerged. The people bowed to receive the customary blessing, "The Lord bless thee, and keep thee: the Lord make His face to shine upon thee, and give thee peace," but he uttered not a word. They crowded round, but Zacharias could only motion to them by signs. With difficulty he managed to convey to them that a vision had been given him as he ministered, but of its nature they could learn nothing.

Despite his handicap, Zacharias stayed to complete his days of service. Then he returned to the village among the hills to break the wonderful news to his wife. He could say nothing to her, but with a wax writing tablet and pointed metal stylus he was able to tell her of the visit and message of the angel Gabriel.

In deep thankfulness for the honour that was to come to her, Elisabeth went into quiet retreat patiently to await the fulfilment of the promise.

This chapter is based on Luke 1:5-25.

Great News from Nazareth

SIX months had passed quietly by for Zacharias and Elisabeth while they awaited the birth of the forerunner of the Messiah, when one day there arrived a surprise visitor from Nazareth, a little hill town of Galilee some sixty-two miles away. It was Elisabeth's young cousin, Miriam or Mary, and marvellous was the story she had to tell.

Though living in quite a poor home in Nazareth, Mary was a descendant of the royal house of David. She was betrothed to be married to a good man named Joseph, a carpenter, who was also of the line of David, both their families having moved up to Nazareth years before. The time of their marriage had been set, but Mary was still living with her parents, or perhaps with relatives, for her father and mother are nowhere mentioned in the Bible story and may already have been dead. Then one day Gabriel, the angel who had spoken to Zacharias in the temple, appeared to the young maiden. His previous commission for God had been an honoured one, but no angel ever bore so wondrous a message as he now brought.

"Hail," Gabriel began, "thou that art highly favoured, the Lord is with thee: blessed art thou among women." Startled at God's special concern for her, she waited wonderingly as the angel continued, "Behold, thou shalt conceive in thy womb, and bring forth a Son, and shalt call His name Jesus. He shall be great, and shall be called the Son of the Highest," Gabriel went on: "and the Lord God shall give unto Him the throne of His father David: and He shall reign over the house of Jacob for ever; and of His kingdom there shall be no end."

Ever since the prophet Isaiah had penned his inspired promise of the Messiah, "Unto us a Child is born, unto us a Son is given," every maiden in David's line had hoped that she might be chosen as mother of the "Prince of peace," and now at last

---

Mary visits Elisabeth and Zacharias to tell them of the honour that was to be hers.
BY CARL BLOCH

to this trusting maiden came the word that she was to be the favoured one of Heaven. She was to be the mother of David's greatest Son, the Redeemer of men, and the eternal King!

If Zacharias was staggered by the knowledge that his child was to be the forerunner of the Messiah, it is little wonder that Mary was unable to comprehend the mystery of the Incarnation of the Son of God.

"How shall this be?" was all she could say. Gently, and without reproof that she failed to understand this greatest of mysteries, the angel explained, "The Holy Ghost shall come upon thee, and the power of the Highest shall overshadow thee: therefore also that holy Thing which shall be born of thee shall be called the Son of God."

Many since the day Mary received this stupendous news have said, as Mary did, "How shall this be?" but unlike Mary, who in simple faith and deep gratitude for the divine honour, believed God, they have stumbled at the unfathomable miracle of the union of divinity with humanity in the Person of Christ. Some have dismissed the story of the Incarnation as a myth akin to the birth of the sons of the gods in heathen religions. Others have even accepted the accusation of some of the wicked rulers of the Jews that Mary was seduced during the days of her betrothal.

But the Bible account cannot be dismissed as myth, or worse, a deliberate falsehood, for if it were thus torn out of the sacred story the whole fabric of the Christian faith would be destroyed.

If the story of the Incarnation is not true then Jesus was an impostor, His first followers were utterly deceived, and Christianity is the falsest of false religions. But the life, death, and resurrection of Jesus and the birth of the Christian church, which make up the Gospel record, attest that it is true, that Jesus was indeed Emmanuel, "God with us."

Mary's first thought, after the departure of the angel, was to visit Elisabeth in Judea, for she knew of the angel's visit to Zacharias, and they should be told at once of the revelation that had now come to her. So quickly she set out on her journey. When the cousins met, both were carried away with joy at the honour that God had bestowed upon them—the one destined to be the mother of the Messiah, and the other the mother of His herald and forerunner.

"Whence is this to me," cried Elisabeth, "that the mother of my Lord should come to me?" In these words she recognized both the divine and the human nature of the coming One. He would be her "Lord," from heaven, yet He would acknowledge Mary as His "mother."

As Mary listened to the inspired language of her cousin, there burst from her lips a rapturous song of adoration and praise, in which she gathered all that God's prophets of earlier days had said concerning the work of the Christ-Child she was to bear. In later days this song of praise came to be known as the "Magnificat" because it begins, "My soul doth magnify the Lord, and my spirit hath rejoiced in God my Saviour."

For three months Mary stayed with her cousin, and then, just before the fore-runner of Jesus was to be born, she returned to her home in Nazareth.

When the appointed time came, Elisabeth gave birth to a son, just as the angel had told her husband, and naturally all her relatives and friends in the village came along to congratulate and rejoice with her.

The eighth day was an important day in the life of a Hebrew child, for it was then that his name was formally announced and he was officially adopted, by circum-cision, into the nation of Israel. Many guests were invited to the ceremony and, as was to be expected, they wanted to help the parents to choose the right name for the little one. All quickly came to the conclusion that he should be named after his father. Zacharias meant, "Remembered of Jehovah," and certainly God had remembered the prayers of His two godly servants!

When, however, they made known their unanimous suggestion to Elisabeth, she at once objected, "Not so," she said; "but he shall be called John."

Everyone was puzzled at her definiteness and protested that there was no-one in the family who had that name. If it was not to be Zacharias, at least it ought to be a name which was in the family!

Up to this point Zacharias had not been included in the discussion, for he had not spoken since he was visited by the angel, and it seems likely that he had become deaf as well. But now the relatives gathered round and by signs asked him to give the final word.

Motioning for the writing tablet, which had become a familiar object during his months of dumbness, he wrote without hesitation, "His name is John," as the angel had instructed him months before. And to the amazement of all that were in the house, as soon as he had written the words, his tongue was loosed and he cried out in praise to God.

Quickly the news spread abroad. Everyone in the village and far beyond heard of the miraculous healing of the old priest. "What manner of child shall this be?" they said one to another.

Meanwhile Mary had arrived back home in Nazareth. Until now she had said nothing to anyone but her cousin about the divine Child she was to bear. But as the time of her marriage drew near when she would enter the home of her husband, Joseph was told of the sacred responsibility that was to be his.

At first he found it hard to believe the news, so God sent an angel, probably Gabriel, to him in a dream to assure him that Mary's miracle-born Son would be none other than the long-promised Redeemer whom they were to name "Jesus," which means, "the salvation of Jehovah," for, said the angel of the Lord, "He shall save His people from their sins."

Obediently Joseph accepted the honoured part he was to play in caring for the promised Child and His mother. And following the wedding celebrations, he took Mary into his home and tenderly ministered to her as she awaited the birth of the holy Babe.

This chapter is based on Luke 1:26-80; Matthew 1:18-25.

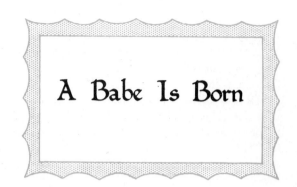

CHAPTER
THREE

A Babe Is Born

SEVEN centuries before Jesus was born, God inspired the prophet Micah to name the very place where He would make His entry into the world. Said the prophet:

"Thou, Bethlehem Ephratah, though thou be little among the thousands of Judah, yet out of thee shall He come forth unto Me that is to be Ruler in Israel; whose goings forth have been from of old, from everlasting."

As Joseph and Mary continued to reside in Nazareth after their marriage, it seemed as if the prophetic announcement must prove wrong, and that Jesus would be born not in Bethlehem of Judea, but in Nazareth of Galilee!

Time and again, however, we read in the Bible the significant words, "The Scripture must needs be fulfilled." And once more, in spite of all appearances, this was to happen.

Just at the crucial time when Mary's Child was to be born, the quietude of Nazareth was disturbed by a decree from Cæsar Augustus, emperor of Rome, ordering a census or registration throughout the Roman world. In most Roman provinces the people registered in the city where they lived, but in Palestine, where the tribal descent was so esteemed, the Romans made a concession to the custom of the country and ordered all to go to the place of their birth to register. Incidentally, the same practice was adopted for the census in Egypt and in Gaul.

Now it will be remembered that though Joseph and Mary had always lived in Galilee, both were of the royal family of David, and as David's city was Bethlehem, it was there that they had to go. So the command of the emperor in Rome, all unknown to him, fitted in most wonderfully with the gracious purpose of God!

Actually the timing of the census in Palestine was even more remarkable than appears at first sight. It seems that the original instructions had been issued by the

Joseph, like Mary, was of the royal line of David.
By GUIDO RENI

21

Emperor some three years before, and if they had been acted upon immediately by King Herod the Great, it would have taken Joseph and Mary to Bethlehem even before they were betrothed! And then there would not have been another census for fourteen years!

It was because Herod feared the census would cause trouble among the Jews, who were already smarting under the tyranny of Rome, that he decided to postpone it for some time, and so it came to be issued just in time to bring Joseph and Mary to Bethlehem for the birth of Jesus. Was it a coincidence? Surely not. Rather was it according to the plan of God "who worketh all things after the counsel of His own will."

For the purpose of the census it was only necessary for the head of the family to go to his native town, but Joseph must have recognized that the summons was in the providence of God and so, in spite of the burden of such a journey to Mary, he decided to take her with him, and she readily agreed to go.

Usually when Jews were travelling from Galilee to Judea they avoided the direct route through Samaria because of the bitter hostility between the Jews and the Samaritans, preferring to take the longer route through Perea on the other side of the Jordan. But on this occasion, to make the journey as easy as possible for his wife, Joseph most likely took the road south through Samaria and then over the rugged moorlands of Judea to Jerusalem. Travelling gently, with Mary riding on the back of a donkey and Joseph walking by her side, they would be on the road for about three days, and it was quite late on the third day that they passed by Jerusalem on the last five miles of their journey.

Along the Hebron Road still southward Joseph trudged, dusty and weary, urging the donkey before him. Mary was tired, too, and both longed to reach their destination.

Reaching a hilltop near the ancient tomb of Rachel, the wife of Jacob, their goal came into sight at last. There were the white houses of the little town of Bethlehem clustering on the crest of a ridge overlooking a fertile plain which stretched away eastward to the parched and barren hills of the wilderness of Judea.

With weary steps they pressed on up the hill into the town, but when they reached the only inn which Bethlehem could boast, they found it filled to capacity by the unusual number of visitors.

At such a late hour Joseph knew it would be useless to seek other lodgings on the dark and narrow streets, so he asked if any place around the inn, however humble, could be found for Mary and himself. The innkeeper could only suggest that they make themselves as comfortable as possible in one of the cave-like rooms cut into the side of the hill, where the animals were tethered. Grateful for even this poor shelter, Joseph conducted his wife to one of them and prepared a place upon the straw for her to rest. And only just in time, for that very night Jesus was born: There He was wrapped in swaddling clothes, like every Hebrew baby of those days, and laid in the manger of a cattle stall.

If the innkeeper had known that the Saviour of the world was to be born in his house, he surely would have made the very best room ready to receive the new-born Babe. The guest who had booked the room would gladly have moved out. It would have been something that both would have talked about as long as they lived. But their ignorance of the momentous event was also according to the plan of God. Jesus came into the world by the humblest of parents and in the lowliest of places to show that none would ever be too humble or lowly to share in His love.

If Jesus had been born in a gilded room in a great palace and had been laid in a costly cradle, the poor people would have felt that a great gulf was fixed between Him and them. So it was not to a palace but to a stable, not to a costly canopied cradle but to a cattle-stall, that He came. He who owned "the cattle upon a thousand hills" chose to be born in a manger. From Bethlehem, "the house of bread," came forth He who was to be the "Bread of life" to men.

The centuries that have passed since that night have changed Bethlehem greatly. The inn has long since gone, but upon the spot where it stood rises the oldest Christian church in the world! At the east end, two narrow flights of stone steps descend to an irregular rock grotto whose low roof has been blackened by the smoke of thousands of candles and lamps. In the cave is a niche hollowed in the wall, and on its marble floor, illuminated by fifty lamps suspended from the roof, is a silver star. There, or somewhere very near it, Jesus was born over nineteen hundred years ago.

On the other side of the grotto is another niche which looks as if it was once a rock-cut manger, perhaps the very one where the little Lord Jesus was laid upon the dry straw.

You may say, But how can we be so sure of the place where Jesus was born? Well, you will notice that the Bible account speaks of "the inn" of Bethlehem, indicating that there was only one in the town. Many of the first Christians would know the inn of Bethlehem, for it must have continued in use for years after the time of Jesus. From their descendants, the Empress Helena, mother of the first Christian Emperor, Constantine the Great, learned of the spot and made it into a little sanctuary. Later, the great Emperor himself raised a beautiful church over it to keep for ever in memory the place of the Incarnation.

While both the outside and inside of the church have been altered many times through the centuries, there are still, on either side of the central aisle leading to the grotto of the nativity, four rows of stone columns which Constantine set up. And for sixteen hundred years Christian pilgrims have passed between them and descended into the cave below to meditate beside the place where the Son of God became the Son of man. Through trap doors in the present floor of the church can be seen the remains of the original mosaic upon which the earliest pilgrims walked to the hallowed spot.

Maybe you will never have the opportunity of going there yourself, but wherever you are, there is something you can do which the innkeeper of Bethlehem failed to do that memorable night long ago; you can make room for Jesus in your heart and life.

This chapter is based on Luke 2:1-7.

CHAPTER

FOUR

While Shepherds Watched

F ROM the hill on which Bethlehem stands, the ground drops steeply down through olive groves and vineyards to a wide, green plain. Beyond rise the bare brown hills of the wilderness of Judea and over the summit ridge one can just see the high plateau of Moab on the other side of the Dead Sea.

It was on this plain that Ruth the Moabitess gleaned among the corn to eke out a living for herself and her mother-in-law, Naomi. Here also David, her great-grandson, was tending the flocks of his father, Jesse, when Samuel came to anoint him king of Israel in succession to Saul. Today barley is still grown on parts of the plain, and sheep graze. About a mile from Bethlehem is a little village called Beit Sahour, which means "the house of the shepherds" or "the house of the watchers," reminding us of what has always been the chief occupation of the dwellers of the plain.

While Joseph and Mary were seeking shelter in the inn, the shepherds of Bethlehem were driving their flocks into the shelter of the stone sheepfolds for the night. Their tents or booths were already set up near the entrance to the folds and while some lay down to sleep, others settled themselves around the camp-fires to keep the first of the four three-hour watches under the star-studded sky.

We are accustomed to thinking of the vigil of the shepherds as being a very cold one in the depths of winter, but really this could not have been so, for sheep were not kept out in the open fields so late in the season. Although Christmas day is traditionally observed on December 25th, the actual time of Christ's birth was more probably some time in early autumn, when the sheep still roamed the valley pastures and the nights were not unduly chilly.

Palestine shepherds in those days did not have a very good name. They were mostly rough and uncultured, and their brute strength, so useful in protecting the

---

The humble shepherds fell down before the manger and worshipped the holy Babe.

By AXEL HELSTEDT   25

flocks from wild beasts, was sometimes turned to acts of brigandage against unwary travellers. But around one of the camp-fires on this memorable night was a group of simple but godly shepherds of David's sort, and as the long hours slipped by the conversation turned to the "blessed hope" of the Messiah which kindled in so many Jewish hearts in those days. The Old Testament prophet had said that He would come forth out of Bethlehem. Would it be in their day?

Suddenly, as they talked, a dazzling light burst upon them. Blinded by its brilliance and transfixed with terror, they fell upon their faces. Then, to their astonished ears, came the assuring words, "Fear not." As they lifted their heads from the ground they beheld Gabriel, "the angel of the Lord," who had spoken those same comforting words to Zacharias in the temple and to Mary in Nazareth.

As their eyes became accustomed to the glorious sight, Gabriel continued: "Behold, I bring you good tidings of great joy, which shall be to all people. For unto you is born this day in the city of David a Saviour, which is Christ the Lord. And this shall be a sign unto you; Ye shall find the Babe wrapped in swaddling clothes, lying in a manger."

No sooner had the angel finished speaking than the night sky was lighted up even more brilliantly by a multitude of accompanying angels praising God and crying in unison, "Glory to God in the highest, and on earth peace, good will toward men."

Then, just as suddenly as the angels appeared, they vanished, and darkness enveloped the fields of Bethlehem once more.

Gradually the full import of the wondrous tidings dawned upon the shepherds. The Messiah had come to David's city and, in response to their faith and hope, God had chosen them, of all the people in Bethlehem, to receive the glad tidings of His birth.

Excitedly they consulted with one another as to what they should do, and it was agreed that they ought to go at once into the village to see for themselves what the angel had told them. Stoking up the fire in front of the entrance to the sheepfold to scare away any wild beast which might come lurking around while they were away, they set off quickly across the fields and up the hill. Led by God, they hurried along the dark streets to the inn and entered the cave-like room where Joseph and Mary had found humble lodging. There they saw the holy Babe wrapped in swaddling bands asleep in a manger, watched over by His mother and Joseph.

Thrilling with joy at the sight, the rough shepherds fell down before the manger and worshipped. Then they told Mary and Joseph of the angel's message and the song of the accompanying throng.

By the time the shepherds left the cave, day was breaking and people were beginning to stir in the inn and the houses around. To them the shepherds narrated the story of their angel visitors and of the Babe in the manger. Soon Bethlehem was buzzing with the news.

Some believed the word of the shepherds, but the great majority, who expected the Messiah to come as a great Conqueror and King, dismissed the story as imagination when they found in the stable nothing more than a newborn Baby and His poor parents. And when the priests of Jerusalem were told, they too pronounced it an idle tale.

So the excitement soon subsided, and Joseph and Mary were left alone to tend the infant Christ and ponder in their hearts the happenings of that momentous night.

Well may we go back in thought to the little town of Bethlehem and the rock cradle of Jesus, and ponder, too. Why should these humble shepherds be the first to learn of His birth? In His wisdom God surely planned it that way, just as He planned for Jesus to be born in a stable, so that the poorest and lowliest who longed for deliverance from oppression and sin would know that He had come for them. Not to those who complacently slept but to those who watched for His salvation did He come. And today, the glad tidings are for all people in every land, whatever their station may be, who yearn for the redemption He came to earth to bring.

In an age from which peace has well-nigh departed, Jesus still brings His peace of mind and heart. In a world so full of violence and hate, there flows to each receptive heart the fountain of His good will and grace.

With more cause even than the angels, we can take up the song, "Glory to God in the Highest," for while they acclaim Him glorious in wisdom and sovereignty, righteousness and truth, we know Him also as the loving Father of our Saviour and Lord.

This chapter is based on Luke 2:8-10.

"I bring you good tidings of great joy," declared the angel to the shepherds.

By P. THUMANN

Dedication in the Temple

AS soon as Mary was well enough to leave the stable cave where Jesus was born Joseph moved to a house in Bethlehem, and on the eighth day, just like every other Hebrew child, Jesus was circumcised and His name was announced as the angel had instructed Joseph and Mary before His birth.

For another month or so Joseph and Mary lived quietly in their Bethlehem home. Then, on the fortieth day after Jesus' birth, the time came for Mary to present herself to the priest in the temple and to redeem her firstborn Son according to the law of the sanctuary. So they set off once more along the Jerusalem road they had travelled so wearily but a few weeks before.

If Jesus' parents had been wealthy they would have taken with them the price of a lamb for a burnt offering and of a dove as a sin offering for the purification of Mary, in addition to the five silver shekels redemption money for Jesus. As, however, Joseph was only a humble artisan, and the redemption money was equivalent to twenty days' wages of a labouring man, they could afford only the humbler offering of two doves. But the "offering of the poor," as it was called, was just as acceptable to God when given with a full and grateful heart.

Just a little while before Joseph and Mary reached the temple a godly old man, named Simeon, came in and took up a position of vantage where he could see all who were passing by.

Like the shepherds of Bethlehem, Simeon had lived for years in holy expectation of the coming of the Messiah. Daily he prayed fervently the common Jewish prayer of his time, "May I see the consolation of Israel," and God had honoured the old man's faith by telling him that he would see the Messiah before he died.

On this particular day as he went to the temple he felt that something momen-

---

The eyes of Simeon and Anna were opened to recognize Jesus as the promised Saviour.

By CHRISTIAN DALSGAARD

tous was going to happen. As he stood in the Court of the Women, watching the coming and going of priests and people, he caught sight of Joseph, accompanied by Mary with Jesus in her arms, dropping the price of their offerings into one of the treasury chests ranged along one side of the court.

He watched them move from the treasury toward the steps leading up to the Gate Beautiful for the priest's blessing. Prompted by the Spirit of God, Simeon recognized what neither the officiating priest nor any of the people passing by understood that the Child which Mary carried was the "Consolation of Israel," for whom he had watched so long. Going forward as they descended the steps again, he took Jesus in his arms, and lifting up his eyes to God he said, "Lord, now lettest Thou Thy servant depart in peace, according to Thy word: for mine eyes have seen Thy salvation, which Thou hast prepared before the face of all people; a light to lighten the Gentiles, and the glory of Thy people Israel."

Then, as he handed Jesus back to His wondering parents, he gave the first warning intimation of the enmity which would be aroused by wicked men against Him, and of the terrible sorrow which, like a sword, would pierce Mary's heart as one day she would stand by His cross and witness His last sufferings and death.

Just as Simeon ended his prophecy there came into the temple one Anna, a prophetess, who, like Simeon, had long awaited this day. Widowed after seven brief years of marriage, she had devoted her life to God, and now, at the advanced age of at least a hundred years, she had no other interest than to wait for redemption to come to Jerusalem.

As her eyes fell upon the little group in the temple court, and she heard the words of Simeon, she knew too that the realization of all her hopes had come. Like the aged prophet she lifted her voice in praise to God and began to declare to all around the identity of the Child of Mary. Once again there were some who believed, but most passed by thinking they heard only the pious ramblings of an old woman.

Marvelling at these new evidences of the true nature of the Babe whom God had placed in their care, Joseph and Mary completed their devotions and returned to Bethlehem.

What a lesson there is in this temple scene for us. Like the shepherds, Simeon and Anna were watching and waiting, and their eyes were opened to see God at work for the salvation of men. On the other hand, the heedless multitude of priests and people passing by saw nothing, and received no blessing.

Today it is just the same. God is still "working His purpose out, as year succeeds to year." Those who are watching discern His activity in the world and in their own lives. The rest go blindly on their way knowing not that the Saviour is passing by. Oh that we, like Simeon and Anna, may see and recognize Him that He may bring light and consolation to our hearts.

This chapter is based on Luke 2:21-38.

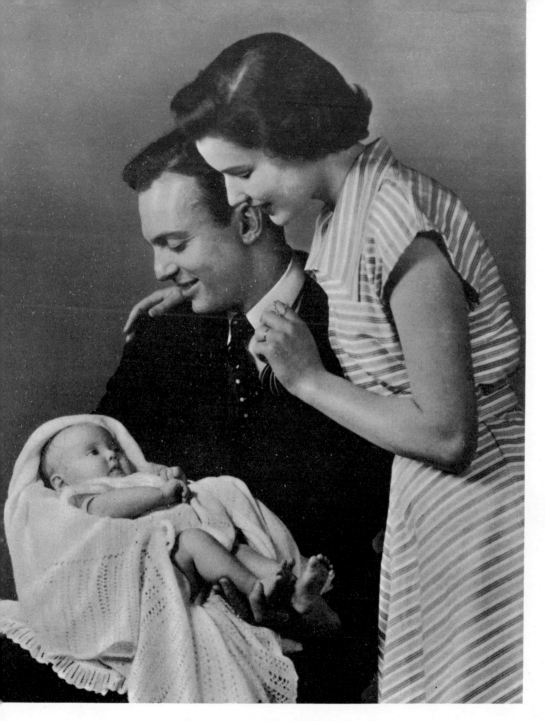

Little ones today may be dedicated to God
as Joseph and Mary dedicated their Child.

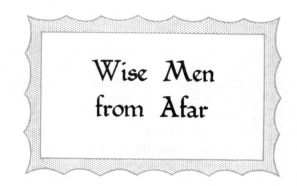

Wise Men from Afar

I T was not long after Joseph and Mary had settled down to their quiet life in Bethlehem, and Joseph had taken up again his trade of carpentry, that they had more visitors to see the holy Child.

This time it was not shepherds who came from the neighbouring fields, nor pious Israelites like Simeon and Anna who waited in the temple for the consummation of their hopes. To their humble home came "wise men from the East," to pay their homage to the infant Christ. We naturally ask, How did they get to know? What was it made them come so far?

It was not so strange as might at first appear, for the expectation of a great Deliverer was not by any means confined at this time to the Jewish people. Millenniums before, when sin first came to Eden, the promise was given to Adam and his wife concerning the "Seed of the woman" who would come to bring deliverance to a suffering and sinful world.

While this promise had been most carefully cherished by Israel, God's chosen people, a vague remembrance of it was handed down even among nations who had fallen into idolatry. So, in many lands, a sense of expectancy was abroad. Even the sceptical Roman writer Tacitus, in his *History,* records the belief that "men would see someone coming out of Judea to govern the entire universe."

In Persia, or Parthia, as it was called at that time, lived the Magi, a wealthy and influential order of priest-philosophers who had a particular reason for being acquainted with the Jewish hopes, for they were descended from the astrologers of ancient Babylon, where the Israelites had lived during the Babylonian captivity. Like the wise men of Babylon, the Magi spent their time studying the heavens, believing that they could read in the stars indications of coming events upon the earth. Many,

The wise men from the East present their costly gifts to the infant Christ.
By J. M. H. HOFMANN

however, were sincere searchers after the true God and were acquainted with the Hebrew Scriptures. These had been impressed by the prophecy of Balaam concerning the "Star" which was to arise out of Jacob and the "Sceptre" out of Israel. Perhaps they had also perused the prophecies of Daniel which were written in Babylonia and Persia. Whatever the source of their information, the devout Magi were constantly scanning the heavens in the hope of seeing this sign of the "Star."

Honouring their sincere, if imperfect, understanding, God granted to the waiting ones, away off among the Gentiles, the sign for which they looked. A mysterious new star appeared in the western firmament. Astronomers have searched the records of the past for some mention outside the Scriptures of a unique celestial phenomenon about this time, and various explanations have been offered. The Bible account, however, suggests that it was not one of the "novæ" or new stars which every now and then blaze up in the heavens, but a celestial light which God caused to shine to attract the attention of those searchers after Him.

Certain it is that they saw something extraordinary and interpreted it as the long-looked-for sign that the Messiah of the Jews was at hand. Excitedly, several of them saddled their camels and set off across the desert for Palestine where they knew the King was to appear.

From the early days of the Christian faith it has been said that there were three Magi in the party, and that they were "kings." But the Bible account simply refers to them as "wise men from the East."

When Abraham travelled from Ur of the Chaldees he took the easy road around the edge of the great Syrian desert by way of Haran. But the wise men doubtless struck straight across the desert from oasis to oasis on their camels until they came to Damascus. Thence they travelled down through Gilead and the Jordan Valley, up the mountain road from Jericho, and over the Mount of Olives to Jerusalem.

In his palace in Jerusalem, Herod the Great was apprised by his spies of the arrival of the picturesque visitors from the Orient, and great was his alarm when he learned whom they were seeking.

"The King of the Jews!" Why that was his own title. Was there a rival for the sovereignty he had received at the hands of Cæsar? He had already foully murdered a number of members of his family, including his wife Mariamne, her brother and her mother, two of Mariamne's sons, his own brother and his uncle, to eliminate any menace from them to his supreme power. Now he must get to the bottom of this new story and crush its instigators with just as ruthless a hand.

First, therefore, he called the "chief priests" and the "scribes," the interpreters of the sacred writings, to ask if they knew anything about this alleged "King of the Jews." Yes, they assured him, the Jewish sacred Scriptures did declare that Messiah would come forth from Bethlehem of Judea. But strangely enough, they never mentioned the wonderful fulfilment of this prophecy in the birth of Jesus. They had heard of the angels' visit to the shepherds and of the Babe born in the inn at Bethlehem, but such a report would have to be on better authority than that of despised shepherds for them to take any notice.

But the information which Herod got from the priests, linked with the sudden arrival of the "wise men," increased his alarm. He felt his throne to be threatened. So he secretly called the wise men and, with apparent courtesy, questioned them as to when and how they had come to discover the star. Then he told them of the prophecy that the Messiah would appear in Bethlehem and bade them continue their inquiries there. If they should get any information about the new King, he said, they were to be sure to bring word back, so that he could go and worship also!

The wise men were apparently quite deceived by the king, and Herod congratulated himself on the subtlety of his plan. If his men were to go openly to Bethlehem, he reasoned, the partisans of the new King would become alarmed and would slip through his net. The wise men, on the other hand, would not arouse suspicion, and when, unsuspectingly, they revealed the hiding place of his rival, he could take swift action.

So the men from the East went on their way. Travelling by night, as was their custom, they were delighted to see the heavenly star again, seemingly going straight before them. Assured now that they were almost at the end of their search they followed the guiding light to the house where Jesus lived, and went in.

They were not in any way taken aback by the sight only of a little Child, for when they made their inquiries they asked, "Where is He that is born King of the Jews?" They were sure that this was He and without a moment's hesitation they prostrated themselves on the ground in Eastern fashion before Him, presenting their costly gifts of gold and frankincense and myrrh.

When the shepherds came to the manger of Bethlehem they represented the poor and humble who in later days "heard Him gladly." But Jesus was the Saviour of the rich and the wise as well, and He was just as ready to receive them and to accept the gifts of their love. Being Gentiles and not Jews, these wise men were also the first representatives of the millions who afterward would recognize Jesus as the Saviour of the whole world.

So, with the coming of the wise men, Jesus had received His tribute of adoration from near and far, from Jew and Gentile, from poor and rich, from simple and wise.

Rejoicing that they had found and worshipped the King, the wise men prepared to return to Herod with their great news. Still they did not suspect Herod's intentions. But God was fully aware of them, and that night, in a dream, He told the wise men to return to their own land by another way without seeing Herod.

There is a road which runs from Bethlehem across the pastures of the shepherds and then down a rugged wadi direct to the plain of Jericho without touching Jerusalem. Without doubt this was the route which they took. And before Herod learned of their departure they were across the Jordan and on their homeward journey.

This chapter is based on Matthew 2:1-12.

Down Into Egypt

HAVING frustrated Herod's attempt to discover the whereabouts of Jesus, God now took steps to remove His Son from the king's wrath. In a dream God warned Joseph of the danger, and instructed him at once to take his family down into Egypt beyond the jurisdiction of Herod until the tyrannical king should die.

Joseph's first thought may have been to make inquiries at the inn and join the next caravan to take the road to the south, but then, realizing that Herod might stop and search any caravans leaving the town, he decided to set off secretly by night.

Hardly had they got away than word came to Herod that the wise men had left without returning to Jerusalem. Furious at the thwarting of his evil plan he ordered the band of ruffians, whom he kept especially for carrying out his brutal and murderous decrees, to massacre all the children under two years of age in Bethlehem, and for some distance around as well, so that his unknown rival might not escape. The number of his victims could not have been as large as is often believed as in a little town of a couple of thousand or so inhabitants there were probably not more than about thirty male children of this age. But though Herod had committed greater crimes, this was a fearful act.

When Joseph and his family reached "the river of Egypt," at the modern village of El Arish, they left the domain of Herod. From there on it was a safe and comfortable journey along the much-frequented "Way of the Sea" to the delta of the Nile.

The Bible does not tell us just where the holy family settled during their brief stay in Egypt, but they would certainly have no difficulty in finding communities of their fellow countrymen. Actually, out of the eight million people in Egypt at that time, no fewer than one million of them were Jews who had migrated there to live.

One of the chief Jewish centres was Alexandria in the Delta. When, following

By night Joseph and Mary, with their precious Child, escape from the wrath of Herod into Egypt.

By OTTO LINGNER

his conquest of Egypt, Alexander the Great built this city and named it after himself, he populated it largely with Jews attracted by the special privileges he offered, and in the centuries that followed it became the greatest Jewish colony· outside Palestine. The Jews controlled most of Alexandria's trade, and large gifts came from the wealthy merchants and bankers there to enrich the temple in Jerusalem.

At Alexandria the Old Testament was translated into Greek for the benefit of the Greek-speaking Jews of Egypt, and this Septuagint version, as it is called, soon became the standard version, both in and outside their homeland, for the Jews who could no longer read the ancient Hebrew tongue.

Alexandria may well have been Joseph's first stopping place in Egypt, but there are reasons to believe that he did not make his home there. For all their generosity to the temple, the Jews of Alexandria were not too well regarded by the conservative Jews of Palestine. Having been subjected for nearly three hundred years to Greek cultural and religious influences, they were rather liberal in their thinking and religious observance.

Joseph, being a devout and conservative Jew with the tradition of the house of David behind him, would hardly feel comfortable in such an environment, and would be much more likely to move on to Cairo where there was another considerable colony of Jews, less influenced by Greek life and thought than the people of Alexandria.

That Joseph did settle there is supported by the many traditions of the holy family in the vicinity. At Mataria just outside Cairo, is the so-called Virgin's Tree, beside which Joseph and Mary are supposed often to have sat. In old Cairo, the Church of Abu Sarga, or St. Sergius, is said to mark one of the places where they spent a part of their exile. Once each year, in the vaulted crypt chapel below the church, the Feast of the Flight into Egypt is celebrated. These are, of course, just legends but, centring as they do around Cairo, they suggest that it was among the Jewish community there that Joseph found shelter and a livelihood during the brief sojourn of the family in Egypt.

Of their life there the Bible tells us not a word, but without a doubt before Jesus left Egypt He looked upon the very pyramids, obelisks, and temple ruins of which the Israelites had such tragic remembrance during their bondage in Egypt. And so yet another of the ancient prophecies concerning the Christ proved true to the letter: "Out of Egypt have I called My Son."

It was in the late autumn that Joseph took his family into Egypt. The next spring, swift judgment came to the infamous King Herod. Contracting a loathsome disease, which racked his body with pain, he sought relief at the hot springs of Callirrhoe, on the east side of the Dead Sea. Finding none, he was brought back to his palace in Jericho where, at the age of seventy, he died. From Jericho his body was taken to another castle, called Herodium after him, a short distance from Bethlehem, and there he was buried in regal splendour.

Surely it was ironical that hard by Bethlehem where he had vainly tried to destroy his most feared rival, Jesus, he should himself, within six months, lie dead!

Until now we have not said anything about the actual date of the birth of the

Child Jesus. The reason is that not until the record of the death of Herod are we provided with definite evidence for the chronology of the early events of His life. But now we are on certain ground, for we know that King Herod the Great died in the month of Nisan, or April, of the year 4 B.C., according to our present dating.

Now Jesus must have been in Egypt since the previous autumn, say October, of 5 B.C., which places His birth in the summer or early autumn of that year. This fits in satisfactorily with the delayed census of Cæsar Augustus, which was originally issued in 8 B.C., and it ties in exactly with the beginning of Christ's ministry at the age of "about thirty years," for which, as we shall later see, we have very specific historical links.

To some it may come as a surprise that Jesus was not born in the year A.D. 1, as our Christian era is supposed to date from the Incarnation. The discrepancy is very simply explained. It is due to a mistake of something over four years which the sixth-century Roman monk, Dionysius Exiguus, made when he established the starting point of our era, and which has never since been corrected.

On the death of Herod, God gave Joseph in Egypt another dream, actually the third he had received relating to Jesus, telling him that it was now safe to return to Palestine. And soon the little family was on its way.

As the angel had not told Joseph in his dream where to go, he decided to return to Bethlehem. This was natural, for having lived there for a while after the birth of Jesus, he must have made friends and contacts in his carpenter's trade. But when he reached the borders of Judea he learned that Archelaus, who had succeeded his father, was as bad as, if not worse than, Herod. So questionable a character was he, even in Rome, that Cæsar gave him only half Herod's domain and made him ethnarch rather than king. The kingship was to come to him if he proved himself worthy, but actually, he had to be removed by Rome because of his brutality in A.D. 6., and was exiled to Gaul for the rest of his life.

No wonder, therefore, that Joseph abandoned the idea of re-entering Judea and instead continued along the great northern highway to Cæsarea, and over the Carmel range to Nazareth. This city was in the tetrarchy of Herod Antipater, an elder brother of Archelaus. He was no paragon of virtue, but he was at least one degree better than his brother.

On the face of it, the return to Nazareth seemed the result of a last-minute change of plans, and quite unintended by Joseph, but even this had been foreseen by God. Centuries before, the prophets had not only declared that Messiah would be called forth out of Egypt, but also that He would be "called a Nazarene."

So it came about that precisely "according to plan," Jesus spent the rest of His childhood days in Nazareth. Does this not assure us that the God who so wonderfully worked out His purpose in the life of our Lord, is equally ready to guide our lives in ways of blessedness if only we will let Him?

This chapter is based on Matthew 2:13-23.

Childhood in Nazareth

NAZARETH, the childhood home of Jesus, is beautiful for situation. It lies in a little amphitheatre among the foothills of Lower Galilee, produced by the widening of one of the rugged valleys which descend to the plain of Esdraelon. It is about sixty-two miles north of Jerusalem and 1,500 feet above sea level. The little flat-roofed white houses climb the slopes of the surrounding hills, interspersed with groves of olive and fig trees and with cactus hedges separating the little plots of ground between the humble dwellings. Beyond the houses rise grassy slopes with scattered limestone outcrops and bedecked in spring and early summer with a profusion of flowers.

Somewhere among the crowded houses of the little town was the home of Joseph and Mary and the Child Jesus. Whether it was on the spot where now stands the Church of the House of Joseph we cannot know, for Joseph's humble home could not have been conspicuously different from all the other similar houses around.

The outer room opening onto the road was built against the side of the hill and served as a carpenter's shop for Joseph. Another chamber on a slightly higher level and dug back into the hillside was the living room of the family, lighted by the outer door in the daytime and by a dim lamp at night.

The furnishings were of the simplest. A low stand in the centre supported the common family dish at meal times. Vessels for washing, drinking, and the preparation of food were ranged upon a ledge around the walls. In a recess were piled the neatly-rolled coloured rugs in which the members of the family wrapped themselves at night. A painted wooden chest by the wall held all the other possessions of the household.

As a little Child, Jesus would often accompany His mother, a water pot on her

In the workshop of Joseph, Jesus learned the carpenter's trade.
By H. LE FOND

head, down to the village spring which bubbled up a few minutes' walk away among the terraced gardens of the valley. This spring still provides water for the village and none can go down to the Virgin's Fountain today without the consciousness that he is walking in the very footsteps of Jesus.

When He was not with His mother, Jesus would watch Joseph fashioning the simple wooden yokes, ploughs, and other tools used to till the fields and cultivate the vineyards and the orchards around Nazareth.

In spring and summer, as He grew older, He would often climb the sunny slopes around the little town to gather flowers and watch the birds as they flitted among the rocks or soared aloft into the sky. There He would see the sower sowing his stony terraced fields, and fondle the lambs as He talked to the shepherds. It was on such occasions as these that He began to gain impressions of the beauties of nature and the bounties of nature's God which were to provide Him with so many of His wonderful spiritual lessons in later days.

Sometimes He would climb right up to the upper rim of the basin in which Nazareth lay, to gaze out into the wide world beyond. And what a scene met His eyes as He stood there looking down upon the plain of Esdraelon hundreds of feet below. It was one of the most beautiful in the whole of Palestine.

Seventeen miles away to the west across the plain, green with springing grain or golden with waving corn, rose the ridge of Carmel, where Elijah had proclaimed the name of God amid the idolatries of his day. Beyond, he could see the glint of the sun on the Great Sea over which sped ships to and from Rome, the mistress of the world.

On the wide plain at His feet many a great event in the history of Israel had been enacted. Sisera had fled across it before Deborah and Barak, and there Gideon had defeated the Midianites. King Josiah died upon it opposing the advance of the armies of Egypt from the plain of Sharon.

Now along the same road that the Egyptians had followed over the shoulder of Carmel, Roman legions from Cæsarea, flaunting their eagle ensigns, marched east-ward to the desert outposts of the empire. From the opposite direction, through Galilee, came caravans of merchandise from Damascus and beyond, bound for Egypt or to enrich the metropolis of Rome.

To the south-east of Esdraelon lay the bare hills of Gilboa, where Saul had fallen before the Philistines. At their base Jesus could see the green Valley of Jezreel descending into the deep cleft of Jordan. There, too, lay the historic towns of Jezreel, Shunem, and Endor, and beyond the slopes of Mount Tabor, five miles away, He could see the high, brown plateau of Gilead on the other side of Jordan.

Looking north across Nazareth from His elevated viewpoint, His view was hemmed in by the plateau of Upper Galilee, whose luxuriant valleys supported innumerable towns and a large population. The Sea of Galilee was out of sight behind the hills, but on a clear day Jesus could just descry the summit of Mount Hermon, the most southerly peak of the Lebanon mountains.

It was as if a map of Israel and the history of the ages was spread out before Jesus as He stood and looked!

The rough steep hills overlooking Esdraelon compelled the great highway of the Via Maris or "Way of the Sea," to turn away to the east, so that the little town of Nazareth was always a secluded spot on a by-road. It is not mentioned once in all the Old Testament record, nor does Josephus, the historian of Jesus' day, refer to it in his list of 200 Galilean towns. It was, as it were, in the midst of the world, yet hardly of it. In what place more fitting than this haven of peace could God's beloved Son have grown up until the time of His manifestation to Israel and the world?

In the days of Jesus the Jews reckoned no fewer than eight stages of development in the life of a young Israelite. But being so distant from the capital, the childhood training of Jesus would be much less rigid and formal than that of the youth of Jerusalem. It was, in fact, one of the complaints of the Jews of Judea that the Galileans set too little store by the traditions of the south. This providentially spared the parents of Jesus from conformity with all the multiplicity of rabbinical ordinances and left Mary free to follow the guidance of God in her Son's upbringing and education.

An atmosphere of love and devotion pervaded the Nazareth home. Daily prayers rose to God in family worship, and the advent of the weekly Sabbath was reverently heralded by the lighting of the Sabbath lamp, prayers, and the special Sabbath evening meal. Family devotions similarly marked the close of the holy hours.

There were other children in the home of Jesus. The Bible mentions that He had four brothers, James, Joses, Simon, and Judas, and several sisters. From later references to them, it is clear that they were all older than Jesus and were children of Joseph by a former marriage. Probably they were already grown up when Jesus began to learn His earliest lessons at Mary's knee.

As soon as He could understand, Jesus would begin to learn the simple promises of the Word and say His first prayers to His Father above. At the age of five the Hebrew child's formal education began. In the larger towns the children could attend the synagogue school, but as Nazareth was little more than a village, Jesus' instruction would be continued by Mary for much of His early life.

From five to ten, His lessons would consist almost exclusively of memorizing the Old Testament Scriptures. Beginning with the books of Moses, and continuing into the prophets and other sacred writings, He would learn long passages by heart. thus laying the foundations of that profound knowledge of the Scriptures that enabled Him to say on any needed occasion, "Have ye not read?" He would also learn the Jewish creed or "Shema," consisting of biblical quotations summarizing the essentials of Israel's faith. And certainly He would recite with ease many of the "hallels," or psalms of praise.

Besides reading and memorizing, Jesus would learn to write, and, as with the oral teaching, the first words He penned would be the words of Scripture.

Plates On Next Two Pages: Page 44. Ain Karem, believed to be the birthplace of John the Baptist. Page 45. In Palestine today many still travel in the same manner as they did in the days of Jesus.

At the age of ten the Jewish child began to study in the synagogue school, or "House of the Book," the rabbinical interpretation of the law contained in the "Mishna." Whether Jesus made His first acquaintance with the traditional scribal lore in this way we are not told, but He must have acquired in His youth a wide knowledge of it, which enabled Him later to challenge convincingly the teachings of the priests and official interpreters of the law.

In addition to His formal instruction, Jesus' knowledge of the Scriptures

ABOVE

Jesus learned His earliest lessons at His mother's knee.

By IRLAM BRIGGS

RIGHT

After lessons Jesus often went to watch Joseph at work in his carpenter's shop.

By IRLAM BRIGGS

OPPOSITE

As Jesus roamed the fields among the beauties of nature, did the thought ever come to Him that He was to be God's Lamb?

was rapidly extended by attendance at the Sabbath and other services in the synagogue. Sitting in the back seats with other children, He would see the rolls of Scripture brought out of the sacred "Ark" and hear the prescribed sections of the law and the prophets read by invited members of the congregation.

Closely He followed the explanations of the Word in the Sabbath sermons, and soon He began to distinguish the unadulterated Word from the fantastic webs of speculation and surmise with which the preachers oftentimes obscured the sacred story.

Outside His daily studies and the devotions of home and synagogue, Jesus shared a happy, active life with the other children of His own age in Nazareth. We may be sure that none was more ready than He to help in the work of home and shop, and we can imagine how eagerly He learned from Joseph to use the axe and saw and plane which gave Him, in His early youth, a mastery of the carpenter's craft.

There are, of course, many apochryphal stories of miraculous happenings during the boyhood days of Jesus, but these are entirely frivolous. So far as we know, there was no hint in His early years of the wondrous works which He was later to perform. Yet there was something different about His gentle bearing and happy spirit which left an indelible impression upon all who came in contact with Him. Full of meaning is the brief description of the physical, mental, and spiritual development of Jesus during those childhood years, "The Child grew, and waxed strong in spirit, filled with wisdom: and the grace of God was upon Him."

This chapter is based on Luke 2:39, 40.

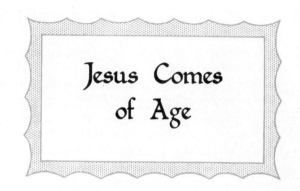

Jesus Comes of Age

A T the age of twelve a Hebrew boy reached one of the milestones on his road to full manhood. By this time he had entered upon what might be described as his secondary education, and, whether rich or poor, he had begun to learn a trade. If of a strict Pharisee family, he would be permitted for the first time to wear on his forehead and arms little leather receptacles or phylacteries containing texts of Holy Writ. And like every adult male in Israel, he was now required to go three times a year up to the feasts in Jerusalem. In his thirteenth year, in fact, he became a "son of the commandment," and thereafter participated fully in the religious life of Israel.

It is extremely unlikely that Joseph presented Jesus with any phylacteries when He reached the age of twelve, but we do know that when the time of the feast of Passover came round that year, he told Jesus that He was to go up with all the other pilgrims to Jerusalem.

The law did not require the women in Israel to go to the feasts as a matter of obligation, but the more devout often went, and it would be very natural for Mary to accompany Joseph on the first occasion that he took Jesus with him.

Many a time Jesus had stood on the hilltop above Nazareth and watched the pilgrim caravan from Nazareth wind its way across the plain of Esdraelon and disappear into the blue distance. How excited He and other boys of His own age must have been as they donned their brightest garments and embroidered girdles and helped to pack the simple requirements for the journey. And when the start was made, we can imagine them running back and forth among the laden donkeys as the crowds of pilgrims stretched out in a long ragged procession along the road.

Which way the caravan travelled on Jesus' first pilgrimage to Jerusalem the

---

Joseph and Mary find Jesus talking with the learned rabbis in the temple.

By CARL BLOCH

Gospel story does not tell us. They may have gone down the fertile Valley of Jezreel and along the Jordan Valley to Jericho, or they may have gone direct through Samaria. Jews travelling north to Galilee invariably took the long way round to avoid the Samaritans, with whom they had "no dealings," but the Galileans did not show the same aversion to their neighbours and commonly went through the Samaritan country.

If they did on this occasion they would cross the Plain of Esdraelon, skirting the flower-strewn meadows and fields and springing corn, and enter the broken hill country of Samaria at Engannim. Along the green valley of Dothan they would wind their way past Samaria and ancient Shechem to Jacob's Well at the foot of Mount Gerizim and Mount Ebal.

Beyond Jacob's Well a toilsome road led up hill and down dale through the country of Mount Ephraim until they reached the high moorland of Judea, so different from the lush pastures of beautiful Galilee.

Normally the journey of sixty-two miles from Nazareth to Jerusalem would be covered in three days, but travelling comfortably they may have been as much as five days on the road.

Reaching the last camp-ground at Beeroth, where the uplands begin to fall steeply southward, the pilgrim party got their first glimpse, in the far distance, of the holy city. What a thrill it must have been for Jesus as He stood by the gate of the ancient khan or among the pilgrim tents and saw the setting sun glint upon the gleaming white marble of the temple.

Arriving next day at their journey's end, they found the olive groves and orchards around the city crowded with temporary booths erected to house the multitudes of pilgrims who had come up for the feast. Jesus and His parents may have sheltered in one of these, or they may have been fortunate enough to find lodgings in Jerusalem itself.

Having settled in they joined with friends from Nazareth in purchasing a lamb for the Passover meal, and daily they were found among the crowds in the temple participating in the Passover services.

Times had greatly changed in Jerusalem since the days of Herod the Great, when Jesus was taken to the temple as a little Babe. After the death of this powerful but wicked king, Cæsar divided his domain into four parts, over which he appointed four of Herod's children as tetrarchs. Archelaus received Judea and Herod Antipas had Galilee and Perea on the other side of Jordan. But Archelaus, as we have mentioned, proved himself entirely unworthy of Cæsar's confidence, and when he was banished for life to Gaul, Judea and Samaria became a Roman province.

Over this newly-formed province Cæsar appointed a procurator. Ordinarily, he resided in Cæsarea on the coast, but in order personally to supervise the crowds at festival time, he would move with reinforcements of Roman soldiers into the capital. From the ramparts of the fortress of Antonia overlooking the temple courts he could keep constant watch to ensure that there was no disturbance.

Little did Jesus realize, as He watched the soldiers patrolling on the walls high above the temple, that one day He would be on trial for His life in that grim fort. For the present, all this was mercifully hidden from the holy Child.

In company with His parents, Jesus wandered here and there among the throngs of worshippers from every part of the Roman world, and of every station of society from richly robed Herodians and phylacteried Pharisees to simple peasant folk. His keen eyes took in every detail of the scene.

From the massive colonnade surrounding the temple area, they made their way through the great bronze gate, which took twenty men to move, into the Court of the Gentiles. Crossing it they came to the double barrier by the foot of the steps which led up to the Court of Women. Here Jesus noticed the warning tablets forbidding, on pain of death, any but Jews to pass beyond.

Through the Beautiful Gate they entered the Court of Women where Jesus watched with interest the worshippers, rich and poor, casting their offerings into the trumpet-shaped openings of the treasury boxes.

Mary could go no further than this court, but Joseph led Jesus up more steps and through Nicanor Gate into the Court of Israel. From there He could look into the Court of Priests where the white-robed priests and Levites busied themselves washing the sacrificial vessels in the great laver and carrying out their sacred duties at the altar of burnt offering, smoking with its perpetual fire.

Beyond, Jesus could see the gilded gate to the sanctuary itself decorated with a great sculptured vine bearing huge golden clusters of grapes.

As with fast-beating heart Jesus watched the solemn services of the sanctuary, did He begin faintly to discern their significance and His destiny?

He turned back again with Joseph to rejoin Mary, glancing, as He passed, through many an open doorway around the courts. In some He saw young students sitting around the rabbis and listening to discourses upon the sacred law. He would have loved to enter and listen, but dutifully He stayed with His parents and joined in their devotions.

How long Joseph and Mary remained at the feast is not clearly stated. The record is that they "fulfilled the days" of the feast. This could mean that they stayed the whole week of the Passover, or they may have kept only the first two obligatory days, the fifteenth and sixteenth of Nisan, when the Passover lamb was eaten and the wave sheaf offered. From what soon transpired it would seem that Joseph and Mary planned to leave on the seventeenth. But Jesus could not tear Himself away, and as His parents were setting off with other Nazarenes, He was hurrying through the temple courts to one of the schoolrooms of the rabbis.

How intently He listened and how penetrating were His questions on the meaning of the temple services, and in particular the Passover feast! Perhaps on this occasion Jesus met Simeon, the son of the great rabbinical leader Hillel, Gamaliel, Paul's teacher a few years later, or even Nicodemus, who later became one of His disciples.

In the meantime Mary, travelling with the other women of the pilgrim company, gave no anxious thought as to the whereabouts of Jesus, imagining Him to be with Joseph or with the boys of the party. On the evening of the first day when they camped on the heights of Beeroth, however, He was nowhere to be found. It was then that Joseph and Mary were alarmed to discover that He was not with the caravan.

As soon as the next day dawned they set off back, reaching Jerusalem in the evening. It was too late that night to hope to find Jesus, but on the third morning they set out in search of Him.

After anxious inquiries everywhere they found Him in the temple sitting in the midst of the doctors, both hearing them, and asking them questions." For a moment they stood speechless as they beheld His earnest face and noted the astonishment of the learned rabbis at "His understanding and answers." Then they rushed forward and Mary clasped Jesus to her breast.

"Son," she began, when she recovered herself, "why hast Thou dealt thus with us? Behold, Thy father and I have sought Thee sorrowing."

"How is it that ye sought Me?" Jesus gently answered. "Wist ye not that I must be about My Father's business?" Joseph might be His earthly protector, but God was His true Father and His purpose for His Son's life Jesus must learn.

As never before Jesus had sensed during those days in Jerusalem His true nature, and in this first recorded utterance, He announced His dedication to His life's task.

Much as they knew concerning their Child, however, Joseph and Mary "understood not the saying which He spake unto them." As yet they did not fully realize the mysterious course His life was to take. But Mary added the remembrance of that day to other miraculous happenings which she cherished in her heart.

Satisfied now with His sojourn in His Father's house, Jesus dutifully followed His parents, and soon they were on the road back to Nazareth. There, once more, the divine Boy was "subject" to them in all things.

His schooling was now more or less over, and Jesus doubtless applied Himself diligently to learning the carpenter's trade. As we hear nothing more of Joseph after the visit to the Passover, it seems likely that he soon died, and as the older brethren of Jesus doubtless married and moved into their own homes, Jesus became the head and bread-winner of the household.

Upon this picture of Jesus the Carpenter of Nazareth the curtain now falls for eighteen long years. Unobtrusively He lived, a devoted Son, a competent craftsman, and a good neighbour in Nazareth. As yet He wrought no wondrous work. He gave no sign of His destiny. He worshipped regularly in the local synagogue, but offered no challenge to the teaching of the rabbis.

Yet these silent years were not wasted. For while, like the good Son that He was, He supported and tenderly cared for His mother, He was in constant communion with His Father above. In His favour and grace He "increased in wisdom" and spiritual "stature" as He prepared Himself for the day when He would take up the work He had come to do.

This chapter is based on Luke 2:41-52.

God Prepares
His Messenger

WHILE Jesus was growing up in Nazareth of Galilee, John, the son of Zacharias and Elisabeth, just six months older, was passing through a sturdy boyhood among the hills of Judah. Of the early years of the child of Mary we know little; of John we know even less. All that the Bible tells us of his years of preparation is contained in one verse, "And the child grew, and waxed strong in spirit, and was in the deserts till the day of his showing unto Israel."

As his parents were already old when John was born, it is hardly likely that they lived beyond his childhood. In the few years that they were spared, however, we may be sure that they followed the instructions of the angel as to the manner of his upbringing and in due time revealed to him the miracle of his birth and his high calling in the purpose of God.

Many have wondered whether John and Jesus met on that memorable occasion when Jesus was brought to Jerusalem for His first Passover, or at any later time, but the Bible gives no hint that they even saw one another till they were both grown men.

It was doubtless when his parents died that John was instructed by God to leave the old home and retire into the desert region of Judea to prepare for his momentous task. So one day found John packing his few simple belongings in his sleeping mat, and setting off over the hills and down into the barren waste of tawny ridges and valleys which drop away nearly 4,000 feet into the deep rift of Jordan.

In the deep jagged gullies of this limestone wilderness, appropriately called Jeshimon or "devastation," were innumerable caves which provided shelter for wild goats and jackals, and also for the robbers who preyed upon lonely travellers on the Jericho Road. In one such cave, probably near some little watercourse, John made his humble home.

He was by no means the first of Israel's prophets to find solitude and communion with God in this wild region. Jeremiah's home was at Anathoth which looked down upon the wilderness a little to the north of Jerusalem. Amos had lived in Tekoa, east of Hebron, overlooking the tangle of hills which descend to the shores of the Dead Sea. Often they, too, must have left their village homes to commune with God in the silent wastes.

Even before the days of John, an austere Jewish sect, known as the Essenes, had established several communities in this wilderness. It was one of these or some similar desert sect who, in later troublous days, hid their sacred scrolls in the caves of the Wady Feshkhah, south of Jericho, where they remained until they were discovered by wandering bedouin a few years ago and given back to the world as the Dead Sea Scrolls, the oldest known copies of the Old Testament Scriptures.

The wilderness of Judea at this time was, in fact, the sanctuary of many in Israel who sought, in nature's solitudes, to escape from the worldliness and hypocrisy of the religion of their day. And who knows but what some saw a new vision of God through contact with John during those years of obscurity?

From the description of John when he began to preach we can picture the manner of his desert life. He wore none of the gaily coloured robes and embroidered girdles of the town-dwellers. His garb was of rough camel's-hair cloth, woven perhaps by his own hands, and his girdle was a length of untanned sheep or goat skin. His hair was uncut, his skin bronzed by the burning sun which beat unremittingly down upon the parched hills.

The sole furnishings of his cave shelter were a water pot filled at intervals from the nearest watercourse, and one or two other earthenware vessels to hold his meagre store of dried pods from the locust or carob tree, called "St. John's bread" by pilgrims in later centuries, and wild honey from honeycombs he found among the rocks.

From his priest father he doubtless inherited some scrolls of Sacred Writ, and to these, when his daily foraging expeditions were over and the simple household tasks performed, he gave himself in study and prayer. So, as the years passed, he grew not only to hardy manhood, but also "strong in spirit." In the quiet of the wilderness he learned more of spiritual things than ever he could have acquired at the feet of the erudite rabbis in Jerusalem. And in communion with God the consciousness of his divine mission intensified into a "burning flame."

At last the time ordained of God for him to announce the coming of the Messiah arrived and "the word of God came unto John the son of Zacharias in the wilderness."

Nowhere in the whole of the Scriptures have we more convincing evidence of the precision of the plans of God than in the way in which they pinpoint the time of John's call. In his gospel, Luke tells us that it was "the fifteenth year of Tiberius Cæsar, Pontius Pilate being governor of Judea, and Herod being tetrarch of Galilee, and his brother Philip tetrarch of Ituræa and of the region of Trachonitis, and Lysanias the tetrarch of Abilene, Annas and Caiaphas being the high priests."

History records that Tiberius succeeded his foster-father—Cæsar Augustus, who had ordered the census at the time Jesus was born—in August, A.D. 14, so that the

GOD PREPARES HIS MESSENGER

fifteenth year of his reign would run from the summer of A.D. 27 to the summer of A.D. 28. Pontius Pilate, the fifth procurator of Judea since the banishment of Archelaus, entered upon his period of office in A.D. 26, and so was in his first year. At this time, too, we know from the Scriptures that Herod Antipas was ruling in Galilee, and that in Jerusalem, Annas was the high priest emeritus and Caiaphas, his son-in-law, the official holder of the office.

Now centuries before, God had given a wonderful prophecy to Daniel in the court of King Darius after Babylon had fallen to the Medes and Persians, in which He declared that from the time that the King of Persia would give permission for the rebuilding of Jerusalem and the restoration of the Jewish state, sixty-nine weeks of years, or 483 actual years, would pass before the Messiah should appear. That decree, which is referred to in the seventh chapter of the book of Ezra, went out in the year 457 B.C., and calculating 483 years from then we come to A.D. 27, the precise year that John was sent forth by God! Isn't that wonderful? The moment the "fullness of time" came, God had His messenger ready to give the momentous announcement that was due. Truly God's promises never fail, and He always keeps them on time!

This chapter is based on Luke 1:80; 3:1, 2.

Out of the wilderness came John the Baptist to announce the coming of the divine Redeemer, the Lamb of God.

By F. SHIELDS

CHAPTER ELEVEN

A Voice in the Wilderness

EAVING his home among the desert hills at the command of God, John descended to one of the fords of Jordan, across which a constant stream of traffic flowed between Judea and the regions to the east. There he began to proclaim the imminent coming of the Messiah, and call Israel to repentance and faith.

Quickly his fame spread abroad as travellers passed on the news. Soon crowds were flocking to hear him, townsmen and country folk, rich and poor. And those who responded to his appeal, "confessing their sins," he led down into the waters of the Jordan and baptized them with the "baptism of repentance for the remission of sins."

It has been suggested that the year when John began to preach was actually a Sabbatic year, when the land lay fallow and business was slack. If this was so, it must have been in the providence of God, that the multitudes would be free to leave their homes and work to come to hear him.

Just which of the many Jordan fords John chose to begin his ministry we do not know for certain. The apostle John, in his gospel, calls the place Bethabara, which means "the house of the crossing."

If he chose the ford nearest to his cave shelter in the wilderness of Judea, it was most likely the one near Jericho, where Israel entered the promised land. Actually, it is here that the oldest traditions have placed the opening scenes of John's ministry.

A few miles before it enters the Dead Sea, the muddy Jordan is some eighty yards wide, but barely a yard deep. It flows through a tropical jungle hemmed in by fantastically eroded limestone cliffs. Willows, acacias, and tamarisk trees overhang the swiftly flowing waters, while flowering reeds and other water plants push out into the stream wherever the curving banks form quiet pools. Innumerable birds dart to and fro over the river and the cool water tempers the heat of the furnace-like gorge.

Beside one of the Jordan fords John the Baptist began to proclaim the coming of the Messiah.

Whether the open space at Mahadet el-Hajlah, to which thousands upon thousands of pilgrims have come to bathe, and where, as early as the fifth century, the memorial church of St. John the Baptist was built, was the scene of John's ministry, we cannot know, but certain it is that in some such natural sanctuary near here the multitudes gathered to listen to the message of John.

Many who came to hear him were at first sceptical about the new prophet. For years the nation had been in constant expectancy of the Messiah, and within John's own lifetime probably a dozen self-styled messiahs had come and gone. Most had been promptly arrested and executed by the Romans for inciting the people to revolt. Was John "the Baptist" just another of these false prophets, or was he Messiah's true forerunner?

When they came and listened they recognized at once that he was unlike the spurious prophets they had known. Here was no fanatical zealot calling them to arms to free themselves from servitude to the Roman oppressors. John directed their minds to their spiritual bondage and urged them, like Elijah of old, to "repentance for the remission of sins." He seemed not concerned so much about the restoration of their national independence as to declare that the "kingdom of heaven" was at hand.

It was a common requirement for proselytes to be baptized into the religion of Israel, but the children of Abraham had never felt they needed anything more than the Levitical washings enjoined by Moses. John, on the other hand, called them to be baptized into the fellowship of the coming Messiah which none could enter through privilege of birth, but only through confession and repentance and faith.

When they asked of John, "What shall we do?" he advocated no revolutionary acts. Instead he bade the tax-gatherers carry out their duties honestly, the soldiers to maintain order without misusing their power, and all to live sincere lives, help the needy, and patiently wait for the coming One.

This prophet was indeed different from any they had heard before. Only dimly did they comprehend the implications of his message, but instinctively they felt that this must be the true forerunner of the Christ!

Among the crowds that surrounded John at the ford of Jordan, however, there were also spies from the Pharisees and Sadducees in Jerusalem who wanted to find out who this rival preacher was that dared to usurp their teaching office and draw away disciples after him.

The Sadducees were the most powerful ecclesiastical party in the days of John and Jesus. Regarded by the Pharisees as liberal in their theology and worldly in their manner of life, they nevertheless had worked their way into the favour of the Herods and gathered to themselves supreme spiritual power. The house of Annas had inherited the high priesthood, and Caiaphas, the son-in-law of Annas, now occupied this high office. Most of the other chief appointments in the temple administration had also been given to members of the Sadducean party.

The Pharisees, at the other extreme, were the ultra-conservative ritualists. They claimed to be the authoritative interpreters of the law of Moses and required of their followers punctilious observance of the innumerable ordinances with which they had surrounded the Levitical law. If the Sadducees had sacrificed the truth of God upon the altar of power and gold, the Pharisees had reduced religion to a burdensome externalism, symbolized by the phylacteries which they wore prominently between their eyes and upon their left arm, nearest the heart.

Between them they had utterly corrupted the worship and service of God and now they were fearful lest their power should be undermined by this new prophet from the desert. So they sent some of their number to mingle with the crowds, and even to request baptism of John. By doing this they thought to dissipate any feeling on the part of the people that the leaders in Jerusalem were in opposition to John. Then, at their leisure, they could decide whether he was dangerous or not, and take appropriate steps to silence him.

But while the common people gave deference to the distinguished visitors and made way for them to come close to the prophet, John was not deceived. From their countenances he detected that they were not there to learn, but to get evidence which they could lay before the Sanhedrin, and perhaps even denounce him to the Roman overlords. So to the amazement of the crowds and to the intense chagrin of the hypocritical priests, he tore away their façade of mock humility and scathingly cried:

"O generation of vipers, who hath warned you to flee from the wrath to come? Bring forth therefore fruits worthy of repentance."

"And begin not to say within yourselves," he went on, "we have Abraham to our father: for I say unto you, That God is able of these stones to raise up children unto Abraham." Mere birth could in no way profit those whose lives belied their high calling.

They might claim to be the olive tree of Israel, but, declared John, "Now . . . the axe is laid at the root of the trees," and "every tree which bringeth not forth good fruit is hewn down, and cast into the fire."

God's "fan is in His hand, and He will throughly purge His floor, and gather His wheat into the garner; but He will burn up the chaff with unquenchable fire."

What an indictment of the perverted religion of John's day and what a rebuke, too, to all in our own times who have only "a form of godliness," but deny "the power thereof."

Shamefacedly the Pharisees and Sadducees slunk away defeated, leaving the multitude of the common people with an even more profound sense of the spirit and power of the desert prophet.

This chapter is based on Matthew 3:1-12; Mark 1:1-8; Luke 3:1-18.

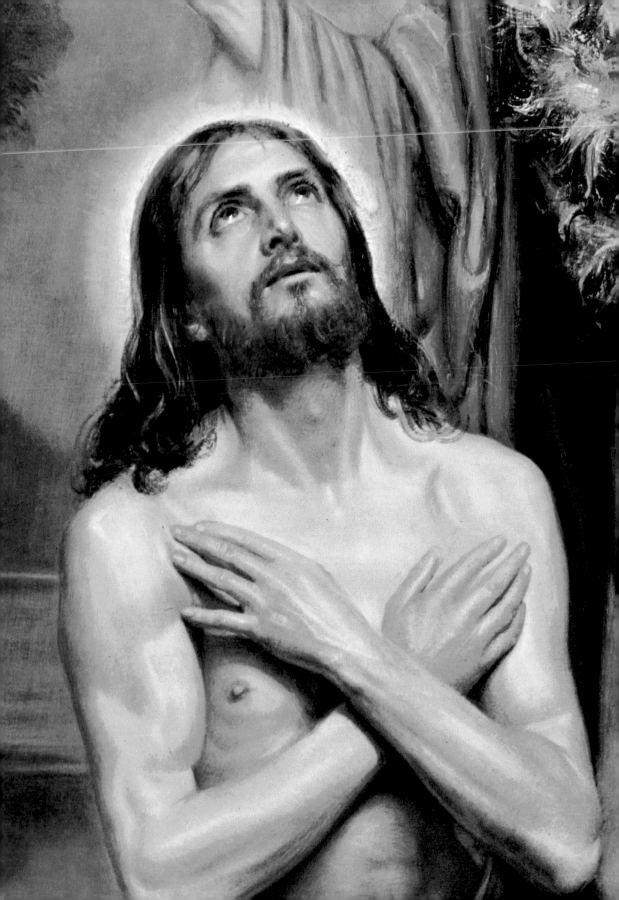

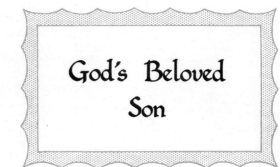

CHAPTER
TWELVE

God's Beloved Son

THE preaching of John at the fords of Jordan raised the crowds who came to listen to a state of intense expectation. On all lips was the excited question, "When will Messiah come?" But even John could not provide the answer. He, too, was waiting.

Without doubt, his parents had told him of the miraculous birth of Mary's Child in Bethlehem, but he and Jesus had never met; nor did he seek any contact with Jesus when he began to preach. All this was in the providence of God, for if they had been in touch with each other, the enemies of the Gospel would certainly have accused them of inventing their story between them.

It was when Jesus heard that John was preaching and baptizing by the Jordan, that He knew the time of His manifestation had almost come.

How long John bore his witness we are not expressly told, but as his ministry began when he was thirty, and Jesus was "about thirty years of age" when the call came to Him, it must have been about six months, for this was the difference in their ages. Then one day in the autumn of the year A.D. 27 the word of the Lord came to Jesus as it had come to John and, bidding good-bye to His mother, He joined the crowds going down to Bethabara, beyond Jordan, where John was baptizing.

As John saw Jesus approaching the impression came strongly upon him that the One for whom he waited had come.

The Bible does not describe their meeting, but we can imagine the emotions which must have stirred in each bosom as John saw the One who had for years filled his thoughts, and Jesus realized that this was the beginning of a road that would lead Him to the cross.

It was Jesus who broke the silence of that first meeting when, to the amazement of John, He asked that He might be baptized.

The prophet recoiled at the idea that the Master should be baptized by the servant.

As He knelt in prayer after His baptism the face of Jesus was bathed in heavenly light.

·By CARL BLOCH

As Jesus came up onto the bank of the river He knelt in a prayer of self-dedication.

By Wm. HOLE

"I have need to be baptized of Thee," he expostulated, "and comest Thou to me?"

Gently Jesus took his hand and drew him toward the water. "Suffer it to be so now," He said quietly: "for thus it becometh us to fulfil all righteousness."

It was not that Jesus had any sin to confess or that He had any need of the "baptism of repentance." He had not. Nor did He need to die on His own account. But just as He was to identify Himself with sinful man, by taking his place on the cross, that through His death we might live, so He identified Himself with man in His baptism, leading the way through the watery grave to newness of life.

John did not understand this at the time, but, unable to resist the gentle authority of Jesus, he "suffered Him," and both went down into the water, and Jesus "was baptized."

As Jesus came up again onto the bank of the river He fell upon His knees in a prayer of self-dedication. John stood reverently beside the kneeling figure while the crowd watched in silent awe. Then, suddenly, as He prayed, "the heaven was opened, and the Holy Ghost descended in a bodily shape like a dove upon Him, and a voice came from heaven, which said, "Thou art My beloved Son; in Thee I am well pleased."

If any of the crowd around Jesus saw the glory which shone in His face, or heard the heavenly announcement, they did not comprehend its meaning. But to John it was a moment of revelation. God had said to him, "Upon whom thou shalt see the Spirit descending, and remaining upon Him, the same is He which baptizeth with the Holy Ghost." When Jesus approached him requesting baptism he felt himself in the presence of the Coming One. When he saw the face of Christ bathed in heavenly light as He knelt upon the bank he knew that He was indeed "the Son of God."

For John the baptism of Jesus and its wondrous sequel was the seal of God upon his faithful witness. It was an assurance from heaven that the Messiah had come!

For Jesus, too, the heavenly vision and utterance were of decisive significance. Angels had announced to Mary before His birth, and to shepherds at His birth, that He was the incarnate Son, and He Himself had testified in His "Father's house" to His divine parentage. Now, in the pronouncement, "Thou art My beloved Son; in Thee I am well pleased," Jesus was assured that His years of preparation had been accepted by God and that He was ready to enter upon His redemptive mission.

On two later occasions God placed a similar seal of approval upon the earthly life of His Son. One was on the Mount of Transfiguration as Jesus entered upon the closing phase of His ministry, and the third was just before He offered His perfect life on the cross.

His anointing with the Holy Ghost at His baptism was significant, too. For by it, as Isaiah had foretold, Jesus was consecrated to His prophetic office. Now He was able to declare, as He did in the synagogue of Nazareth: "The Spirit of the Lord is upon Me, because He hath anointed Me to preach the Gospel." The moment for which the ages had waited had come.

This chapter is based on Matthew 3:13-17; Mark 1:9-11; Luke 3:21-23.

CHAPTER

THIRTEEN

The Conflict Opens

W HEN Jesus rose to His feet on the bank of Jordan after communion with His Father in prayer, John expected that He would declare Himself to the people and that his own work would be accomplished. But instead Jesus, impelled by the Spirit, passed through the crowds and disappeared into the wilderness to seek guidance and power for the accomplishment of His tremendous task.

If Bethabara was somewhere near Jericho, as we have previously intimated, the "wilderness" may have been the confusion of barren hills and wadis to the west of the Jericho plain. Within sight of the ancient city there rises a precipitous limestone peak, honeycombed with caves, known as Jebel Quarantal, which, from earliest Christian times has been pointed out as the place to which Jesus retired. On the other hand, the wilderness may have been the slopes of the mountains of Abarim on the east side of the Dead Sea near Mount Nebo. All we know is that it was in a mountain cave not far from the Jordan ford that Jesus found shelter from the elements and the wild beasts of the wilderness during His lonely vigil.

For forty days He fasted and prayed, precisely the time that Moses spent "without bread or water" on Sinai, and Elijah spent without food on his flight to Horeb. At the end of this period Jesus was composed and resolute as He faced the task which confronted Him, but faint from neglect of His physical needs. Angels of God looked down upon the gradually weakening form of the Son of God, anxious for the command of the Father to hasten to His aid.

Someone else was watching Jesus, too, but with malevolent, not good, intent. Satan had already made one attempt to frustrate the plan of God when he incited Herod to destroy the young children of Bethlehem. On that occasion he signally failed. Now he thought he saw an opportunity of side-tracking Jesus from His mission.

In divine indignation Jesus drove Satan, the tempter, from Him.

By CARL BLOCH 65

So he waited to the end of the long fast and then, when circumstances seemed most favourable, he went in to the attack.

God could, of course, have prevented Satan from taking advantage of the weakened condition of Jesus, but in His wisdom He permitted Satan to do his worst, as in an earlier day He had left the patriarch Job for a time at Satan's mercy.

In His baptism Jesus had portrayed the death to sin and the new birth of the child of God. In His temptation He was to typify the believer's life-long conflict "against principalities, against powers, against the rulers of the darkness of this world." He was to be "tempted in all points like as we are, yet without sin," and in His victory there was to be assurance of ours through Him.

There are, in fact, striking lessons to be learned from the disaster of Adam's transgression in Eden and the victory of the "second" Adam gained in the wilderness.

Satan's temptation of Christ resembled his approach to Eve in that both began on the level of physical cravings or appetite. To Eve, Satan offered the tempting fruit of the tree of knowledge of good and evil. To Jesus Satan said, "Command that these stones be made bread." It was a seemingly inoffensive suggestion. Jesus was hungry after His long fast, and He had the power to change the round cake-like stones scattered around the mouth of the cave into bread to satisfy His physical needs. Then why should He not do so?

For Jesus there were two very good reasons why He should not. In the first place His miracle-working powers were for the blessing of others, not for the amelioration of His own life. He was willing to turn water into wine to bring joy to a young bride. He would multiply a little boy's lunch into enough to feed 5,000 souls who came to listen to His teaching. But He would not work one miracle to supply His own lack. He would rather go hungry than appropriate His divinely-given gifts to His own temporal good.

The second reason was that to have taken matters into His own hands would have been to suggest a lack of care on the part of His Father. He knew God would not allow Him to die before He had even begun His work. He could well, therefore, await God's time and manner for the relieving of His physical needs. Unlike Eve and her husband, and unlike Israel in the wilderness, Jesus was not overcome by the lust of the flesh. Instead He answered, "Man shall not live by bread alone, but by every word that proceedeth out of the mouth of God." So, in His first victory, Jesus pointed the way of trust and obedience to the children of God.

When Satan found that he could not overthrow Jesus by the temptation of appetite, he set a more subtle trap for Him. "The devil taketh Him up into the holy city, and setteth Him on a pinnacle of the temple." This was doubtless the highest point of the temple buildings, on top of Solomon's Porch, from which a priest every morning signalled the first sight of the rising sun and the time for the morning sacrifice.

Standing there with Jesus, looking down upon the multitudes thronging the temple courts, Satan said, "If Thou be the Son of God, cast Thyself down: for it is written, He shall give His angels charge concerning Thee: and in their hands they shall bear Thee up, lest at any time Thou dash Thy foot against a stone."

The suggestion, backed apparently by Scripture, was indeed a subtle one. If Jesus would not use His miracle-working power for His own benefit, surely He would make use of it in any way that would further His mission. If He descended unharmed from the summit of the temple buildings in the sight of the multitudes, His claim to be the Messiah would at once be acknowledged by priests and people.

But again Jesus was not deceived. He was to work many miracles during the course of His ministry, but they would always be to relieve human need, never merely to attract attention to Himself.

Moreover, Satan was misquoting and misapplying Scripture when he used it to trap Jesus, for he changed the words "in all Thy ways" to "at any time," and so completely altered what God had said. The promise was sure to Jesus while He followed the "way" chosen for Him by God, but He could have claimed no protection if He had deviated from it into Satan's "way."

So again Jesus promptly replied, "It is written again, Thou shalt not tempt [or presumptuously put to the test] the Lord thy God."

Foiled a second time, Satan made a last desperate bid to turn Jesus from His purpose. When Satan was thrown out of heaven, God had permitted him temporary occupation of this earth, with the intention of making it the battlefield upon which the controversy of sin would be settled for ever. So Satan, as the "prince of this world," could lay some claim to the disposition of the kingdoms under his control.

He knew that the object of Christ's coming was to defeat and destroy him upon the earth, and to claim the "kingdoms of this world" as His, so he decided to attempt a compromise with Jesus. Says the Record: "The devil taketh Him up into an exceeding high mountain, and showeth Him all the kingdoms of the world, and the glory of them; and saith unto Him, All these things will I give Thee, if Thou wilt fall down and worship me."

What a suggestion! As if Christ would be willing to save Himself the desperate conflict ahead by making terms with Satan which would compromise the whole plan of salvation!

Quickly Jesus exposed Satan's clever plan, and calling the devil now by his right name, Satan, "the adversary," He cried in divine indignation, "Get thee hence, Satan: for it is written, Thou shalt worship the Lord thy God, and Him only shalt thou serve."

Satan's highest bid had failed. The loyalty and the purpose of Jesus could not be subverted. So Satan withdrew from the conflict "for a season," and the waiting angels pressed in to succour and strengthen the weary Son of God.

By His victory Jesus set a shining example of utter trust, self-effacing devotion, and of no compromise with evil, to all who should join Him in the struggle against sin and its author. "Resist the devil," is the message of the temptations of Jesus, "and he will flee from you." May we ever heed that admonition, and in our victory have the consciousness of the ministration of heavenly angels as Jesus had after His great ordeal.

This chapter is based on Matthew 4:1-11; Mark 1:12, 13; Luke 4:1-13.

CHAPTER
FOURTEEN

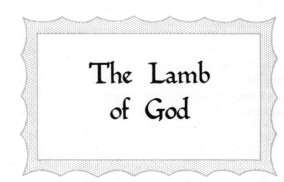

The Lamb
of God

EVER since the Pharisees and Sadducees came down to the Jordan to spy upon John at the beginning of his ministry the Sanhedrin in Jerusalem had become increasingly concerned about the tremendous popularity of the desert prophet.

The news had got around that John had not minced words in his condemnation of their cant and hypocrisy, and they felt that unless they could humiliate him before the people and reassert their authority, their influence would be lost.

So it was decided to appoint an official delegation to go down to Bethabara and publicly interview John.

Pushing their way to the front of the crowd, the deputation opened their attack by superciliously demanding to know if he claimed to be the Messiah. They knew that he had made no such claim, but they wanted to use his public denial to build up their argument that his importance had been grossly overrated.

John did not, however, play into their hands quite so innocently as they expected, for in reply he said, "I am not the Christ." By this he indicated that although he made no claim to Messiahship, he knew where Christ was, and that they would soon have to reckon with Him.

Pretending not to notice the implication of John's words, the priestly questioners proceeded to their next point. "What then?" they said, "Art thou Elias?" It was a common belief among the Jews, as a result of a too literal interpretation of Malachi's prophecy, "Behold, I will send you Elijah the prophet before the coming of the great and dreadful day of the Lord," that this prophet would appear in person to announce the Messiah.

Taking up their question in the literal sense in which his interrogators put it,

---

As the Lamb of God, Jesus was to bear away the sin of the world on the cross of Calvary.

John promptly replied, "I am not," though at his birth it was declared that he would go forth in "the spirit and power of Elias."

"Art thou that prophet?" they persisted, referring to the prophecy of Moses, "The Lord thy God will raise up unto thee a Prophet from the midst of thee, of thy brethren, like unto me; unto Him ye shall hearken." But again John replied, "No."

Feeling that they were getting along very well with their debasement of John the priests went on, "Who art thou? that we may give an answer to them that sent us. What sayest thou of thyself?"

The malignant satisfaction upon their faces was changed to heavy frowns when John answered in ringing tones that could be heard everywhere among the great crowd, "I am the voice of one crying in the wilderness, Make straight the way of the Lord, as said the prophet Esaias."

Earthly kings were accustomed to sending their servants ahead to clear from the rough roads any large stones and other hindrances to their progress. When, for example, Vespasian, the Roman general, afterward emperor, passed on his victorious way through Galilee, he sent ahead a detachment of his troops "to make the road even and straight, and if it were anywhere rough and hard to be passed over, to plane it and to cut down the woods that hindered the march." In like manner, John declared, he had been sent to prepare the spiritual way of the Messiah.

"Every valley," Isaiah had said, "shall be exalted, and every mountain and hill shall be made low: and the crooked shall be made straight, and the rough places plain: and the glory of the Lord shall be revealed, and all flesh shall see it."

To John's claim that he was fulfilling this Messianic prophecy, the priests could think of no reply. So they quickly changed the line of their attack to his authority for baptizing those who responded to his message.

"Why baptizest thou .then, if thou be not the Christ, nor Elias, neither that prophet?" they asked. Surely that was the work of the Messiah Himself. John's baptism was therefore premature and quite inappropriate. But John was ready with his inspired answer. "I baptize with water," that is, symbolically, he declared: "but there standeth One among you, whom ye know not; He it is, who coming after me is preferred before me, whose shoe's lachet I am not worthy to unloose. . . . He shall baptize you with the Holy Ghost."

What was it that John said? the Messiah was not only at hand, but actually standing among them!

Alarm took possession of the priests as they scanned the people around with startled gaze, but they did not recognize Jesus, who had returned from the wilderness and was standing on the edge of the crowd. Hastily they slipped away and hurried back to Jerusalem with their report. There was clearly no possibility of silencing John, and in view of his startling announcement, they must decide quickly what was to be done when the alleged Messiah appeared!

This decisive interview with the religious leaders of the Jews confirmed in John's mind a conviction which had been growing since his first meeting with Jesus.

Until then John had shared the general Messianic expectation of the deliverance of Israel from Roman bondage and the early establishment of the kingdom of the Messiah.

When Jesus, after His baptism, departed without any demonstration into the wilderness, John began to restudy the prophecies of Christ's mission, particularly that penned by Isaiah. His interview with the hostile leaders now finally convinced him that, as Isaiah had so vividly declared, Jesus was to be the divine Sin-bearer before He ascended His royal throne.

The very next day, therefore, when John again saw Jesus mingling with the crowd, he pointed to Him and cried not, "Behold your long-expected warrior King," but, "Behold the Lamb of God, which taketh away the sin of the world."

"This is He," John went on, "of whom I said, After me cometh a Man which is preferred before me: for He was before me. And I knew Him not: but that He should be made manifest to Israel."

Reminding them of the baptism of Jesus, which some of the crowd had witnessed a few weeks' before, he testified: "He that sent me to baptize with water, the same said unto me, Upon whom thou shalt see the Spirit descending, and remaining on Him, the same is He which baptizeth with the Holy Ghost. And I saw, and bare record that this is the Son of God."

Amazed at John's dramatic declaration, the eyes of the people followed his pointing finger and beheld Jesus, His form emaciated after His long ordeal in the wilderness, but with a heavenly radiance shining from a face full of love.

To many the appearance of Jesus came as a shock of disappointment, so different was He from what they expected. But others remembered the words of the Gospel prophet, "He shall grow up before Him as a tender plant, and as a root out of a dry ground: He hath no [royal] form nor comeliness; and when we shall see Him, there is no [kingly] beauty that we should desire Him." Rather would He be "a man of sorrows, and acquainted with grief."

So, by the many, just as Isaiah had foretold, Jesus was "despised and rejected" and they "esteemed Him not." But to the believing few, in that first sight of Jesus, the "arm of the Lord" was mightily revealed. They discerned, as John declared in his wonderful testimony, that Jesus was not only Man, but also the "Son of God."

He had come after John, but He was before him by virtue of His eternal pre-existence. He was the anointed King, yet first He must manifest Himself as the divine Lamb, the Antitype of all the sacrifices back to the garden of Eden, the sinless Substitute who was to bear away, by His death, "the sin of the world."

This chapter is based on John 1:19-34.

The First Disciples

NOW that John had made Jesus known to the crowds by the Jordan, He could very easily have drawn away the people after Him and left the desert prophet feeling desolate and alone. But Jesus was too considerate of John to precipitate any such sudden transfer of loyalties.

As He wended His way down to the river the next afternoon John was not preaching, but talking quietly with two of his disciples. These men were fishermen of Bethsaida, a suburb of Capernaum at the north-western end of the Sea of Galilee. They had come down with many others to listen to John; they had accepted his message and had become two of his most intimate followers. One was named Andrew. The identity of the other is not revealed, but as this touching episode is related only by John it seems certain that it was he.

As Jesus walked meditatively past, John declared again, as he had done the day before, "Behold the Lamb of God!"

From John's manner, it was evident that he felt the time of parting had come, and the two disciples, after a moment's hesitation, left John's side and moved toward Jesus.

Hearing the footsteps of Andrew and John behind Him as He walked, Jesus turned round, and asked them, "What seek ye?" They replied, "Rabbi; (which is to say, being interpreted, Master,) where dwellest Thou?"

"Come and see," Jesus bade them and, leaving the riverside, He led them to the hillside cave or shady copse in which He had found temporary shelter.

The encounter was so unobtrusive that their departure was hardly noticed by any but John. Yet in those few minutes the ministry of Jesus had begun and the first disciples had joined themselves to Him.

Ever since Jesus called His first disciples He has been seeking an entrance into the hearts of men.

By B. PLOCKHORST

It was about the tenth hour when the two disciples spoke to Jesus. Seeing that Judea was now a Roman province, using Roman time, this would be four o'clock in the afternoon. And we are told, "They . . . abode with Him [the rest of] that day."

What an experiencé it must have been! If only we could read that first wonderful discourse which Andrew and John heard from the lips of Jesus. But though no record has been left for us in the gospels, the sequel is evidence enough of the profound impression which Jesus had made. For when they left Him, as darkness fell, Andrew went straight to where he and his brother, Simon, were camped and, bursting in upon him, he breathlessly exclaimed, "We have found the Messias, which is, being interpreted, the Christ."

When Simon heard the news, he was as excited as his brother and could hardly wait till the next morning to meet Jesus. As soon as it was light they were on their way, and soon Simon was being introduced to Jesus. With a penetrating gaze that seemed to look right into Simon's heart, Jesus regarded him, and then He spoke: "Thou art Simon the son of Jona," He said: "thou shalt be called Cephas, which is by interpretation, A stone."

Little did Simon, as he stood there in the presence of Jesus, sense the consequences of that momentous interview. Neither he, nor his brother Andrew, nor John, realized that in giving Simon his new surname, He was symbolically laying one of the first "stones" in the temple of the church which He had come to build, and of which He was the Foundation and Cornerstone.

Jesus knew that impulsive Simon would be a long time before he developed the rock-like quality of character that his new name implied; He knew, in fact, that Peter would almost fail Him in the greatest crisis of His life. But He was also confident that, by God's enabling grace, Simon would be victorious over his weakness and vacillation and become not merely a "stone," but a "pillar" in the spiritual temple of God.

Andrew might have been jealous at the special interest Jesus took in his brother, but he was not. He was happy to have brought someone to Jesus, and too unselfish to envy his brother's selection for a more-notable work than his. Andrew was never to be prominent among the disciples, nor in the inner circle of the companions of Jesus, but he was God's instrument in bringing Peter to Jesus, and he will surely share his reward. And so will many other Andrews among His followers, who live their lives in obscurity and yet may be the means of calling some great worker into God's service.

The Gospel record does not mention whether John sought out anyone to bring to Jesus on this occasion. If his brother had been there we may be sure he would have called him. But James had most likely remained at home to look after the boats, and not until later was he numbered among the disciples.

The day following, Jesus and His three new companions were preparing to leave Bethabara and return to Galilee. Just as they were about to commence their journey they came across Philip, another fisherman. He also was of Bethsaida, the city of Andrew, Peter, and John. Most likely Philip was known to the other three, and when Jesus bade him, "Follow Me," he at once joined himself to the little disciple band.

No sooner was Philip numbered with the disciples than he too began to feel that he should win someone to Jesus, and so before they left he went quickly in search of his friend Nathanael, also called Bartholomew.

Locating his friend in a secluded corner of the fig orchard where he was accustomed to meditate and pray, Philip said to him, "We have found Him, of whom Moses in the law, and the prophets, did write, Jesus of Nazareth, the Son of Joseph."

Nathanael was sceptical, for he actually came from Cana of Galilee, a few miles to the north of Nazareth. He knew how poor a reputation Nazareth had. It was indeed a common saying in those parts, "Can any good thing come out of Nazareth?"

To a deep student of Messianic prophecy as Nathanael' was, there was a further problem. Messiah was to come forth out of Bethlehem of Judah. How then could Jesus of Nazareth be He?

Philip brushed aside Nathanael's doubts by the best possible argument. "Come and see," he urged. And that is the best advice anyone can give to those who have doubts about Jesus.

It is to Nathanael's credit that, while he was sceptical, he was not prejudiced like the rulers of Jerusalem. He very rightly demanded proof of Philip's tremendous claim, but he was ready to accept evidence if it was forthcoming.

As they came within hearing distance, Nathanael heard Jesus saying to His disciples, "Behold, an Israelite indeed, in whom is no guile!" His heart bounded at the generous words, but he was perplexed to know how Jesus could be acquainted with him, seeing that they had never met before.

"Whence knowest Thou me?" he asked. "Before that Philip called thee," replied Jesus, "when thou wast under the fig tree, I saw thee." Nathanael could never remember seeing Jesus, but Jesus had observed him in meditation and study and He knew that Nathanael's heart would respond to His call.

At these words all Nathanael's doubts vanished, and, carried away by emotion, he cried out, "Rabbi, Thou art the Son of God; Thou art the King of Israel."

"Because I said unto thee, I saw thee under the fig tree, believest thou?" Jesus responded. "Thou shalt see greater things than these. . . . Verily, verily, I say unto you, Hereafter ye shall see heaven open, and the angels of God ascending and descending upon the Son of man."

And one day, long after, Nathanael and his fellow disciples did indeed see angels descending to Jesus upon the Mount of Olives to bear Him back to His heavenly home.

This chapter is based on John 1 :35-51.

CHAPTER

SIXTEEN

A Wedding
Invitation

FROM Bethabara at the southern end of the Jordan Valley it was nearly sixty-five miles to Nazareth. The road led first up the Jordan Valley to the ford opposite Bethshan. There Jesus and His five disciples crossed the river and ascended the Valley of Jezreel. Passing the cities of Jezreel, Shunem, and Nain, they traversed the Plain of Esdraelon and ascended the valley leading northward to Nazareth.

Travelling comfortably, the journey would take about three days, and so it was on "the third day" that the little party arrived in Nazareth just about two months after Jesus had left to go to the Jordan. They were just in time to learn of the wedding at Cana and to receive an invitation to be present. At once they continued their journey along the Damascus road over the hill behind Nazareth and reached Cana, between six and seven miles from Nazareth, in the early evening. For many centuries this Galilean town has been identified with the village now called Kefr Kenna, which lies on the fringe of a fertile plain among the Galilean hills, its houses climbing the western slopes surrounded by gardens and pomegranate orchards. Recently, however, archæologists have pressed the claims of the nearby ruins of Khirbet Qana in the plain below.

The family in which the wedding took place must have been close friends of Mary, or she would hardly have taken it upon herself to give instructions to the servants. They may even have been related to her and to Jesus. The fact that Joseph is not mentioned would suggest that he was now dead. Jesus' acceptance of the invitation throws a revealing light upon His interest in family and social life. Despite the solemnity of the task for which He had come, there was nothing austere about Jesus. He mixed with all sorts and conditions of men from the high born and wealthy to

---

Jesus turns water into wine at the wedding feast in Cana of Galilee.

the lowliest, and He was only too happy to join the innocent festivities associated with the wedding of these two young people.

This indeed was to be expected, for at the creation had He not brought together Adam and his wife, and Himself solemnized the first marriage in Eden? Had He not also prepared their lovely garden home? What then could be more appropriate than that the first act of His earthly ministry should be to bless this humble home in Cana of Galilee?

Weddings in Palestine in Bible times always took place in the evening, so Jesus and His party arrived in good time for the wedding service.

As soon as it was dark, the betrothed in bridal array was conducted to the home of her husband by guests carrying torches and floral decorations and to the sound of music.

The local rabbi pronounced the wedding formula, the newly-weds were crowned with garlands, and the legal documents were signed and witnessed. Benedictions then brought the formal service to a close and the wedding feast began. The guests reclined on cushioned couches drawn up around tables on which food and drink were set in abundance. Lamps placed in niches round the room and on the tables illuminated the festal scene.

In families of wealth and high social standing a wedding feast might go on for as much as a week or even a fortnight, but in this humble home it could not have lasted more than a day or two. Even so, it was probably quite a problem to cater for the company assembled. If Jesus and His five disciples were invited at the last minute they may even have thrown out the calculations and contributed to the emergency that Mary suddenly discovered as she superintended affairs behind the scenes.

Hurriedly seeking out Jesus she said to Him, "They have no wine." Just what she expected Jesus to do, we cannot say, for up to this time He had performed no miraculous act. But she knew His sympathy and understanding and was sure that He would do something to allay the distress of the hosts when they discovered the lack.

Jesus' reply, "Woman, what have I to do with thee? Mine hour is not yet come," might seem to our modern ears abrupt. But we know that Jesus never said or did anything to distress anyone, least of all His beloved mother. That He should call her "Woman" was actually not in the least disrespectful. It was a proper form of address in the Orient and was indeed the term which, with infinite solicitude, He used on the cross when He commended Mary to His disciple, John.

And when He said, "What have I to do with thee? Mine hour is not yet come," He was simply indicating, in tones of gentle rebuke, that He could no longer be "subject" to her, but to God alone, and that from His Father He must receive guidance as to what He should do.

Mary was perfectly satisfied by Jesus' reply. She knew He would act in the way His Father directed when the time came, and so she said to the servants, "Whatsoever He saith unto you, do it."

Before long, Jesus approached them in the ante-room as they stood around waiting for further orders. Beside the wall stood six large stone water pots such as are still to be found in modern Galilee. One such ancient pot is treasured in the traditional house of the wedding feast in Kefr Kenna. Each would hold somewhere about fifteen gallons. Obviously they were more than would be needed by any ordinary family and had been brought in by neighbours to meet the needs of the influx of guests.

The pots were now empty, the water having been used by the servants, in accordance with social custom, to wash the hands and feet of the guests before they went in to the feast, and for the cleansing of the domestic utensils.

To the surprise of the servants Jesus bade them, "Fill the water pots with water." Obediently, however, they filled them "to the brim." They were even more surprised when Jesus next said to them, "Draw out now, and bear unto the governor of the feast." But dutifully they went to the pots and began to draw, and out of them came not water, but rich sparkling juice of the grape.

The emotions of the servants are not recorded, but they must have found it difficult to suppress their excitement as they carried the wine to the master of ceremonies. When he tasted it he looked, first at them, and then toward the bridegroom sitting with his bride in the midst of the company. Then he got up and stepped over to him. "Every man at the beginning doth set forth good wine," he said, banteringly; "then that which is worse: but thou hast kept the good wine until now."

The bridegroom was as mystified as the governor that the best wine had been reserved to the end of the feast, for he certainly had given no such instructions. Only the servants, the disciples, and Mary knew that, by a creative act, it had come to them straight from the hand of God.

"This," says the apostle John, was the "beginning of miracles [literally, signs] which Jesus did in Cana of Galilee, and manifested forth His glory."

In this first miraculous act we discern the pattern of all the subsequent miracles of Jesus. They were enacted as "signs" or tokens that He was the Son of God. This first miracle witnessed to His power over nature. Later miracles revealed His power over sickness, over death, and over the devil and his evil minions. Together they showed that "all power" had been given to Him to deliver men from the bondage of Satan and of sin.

But why, we may ask, if miracles were to "manifest His glory," did He not declare Himself at once before all the wedding company? Why indeed did He not choose some more spectacular occasion for the first revealing of His power?

The answer is that the "hour" of His manifestation to the world had not yet come, nor even to the little world of Cana of Galilee. At this time His purpose was to establish the faith of the little band of disciples who were to carry on the work which He was only "beginning" during His brief sojourn among men.

And this first miracle did wonderfully accomplish this object, for we read, "His disciples believed on Him." The faith born of those first contacts with Him by the Jordan was now strengthened into complete trust and utter devotion.

This chapter is based on John 2:1-12.

A Memorable Visit

WHEN the wedding festivities at Cana were over, Jesus' new-found fisherman friends began to feel that they ought to get back to their boats as they had been quite a long while away. At the same time, they could not bear to leave Jesus. What more natural, then, that they should invite Him, with His mother and brothers, to go down to Capernaum and enjoy their hospitality for a few days. The sisters of Jesus were not included as they were doubtless married by this time and would go back after the wedding to their own homes.

Jesus gratefully accepted the invitation and, bidding good-bye to Nathanael, set off with Peter and Andrew, Philip and John. The stony track from Cana passes first through a wide valley of wheatfields and then rises in a long ascent to a high plateau overshadowed by the twin peaks of the Horns of Hattin, famed for its terrible battle in later days between the Crusaders and Saladin.

On the northern rim of this plateau the great basin of Galilee comes suddenly into sight. It is one of the most beautiful views in the Holy Land. On the western side the green hills fall steeply one to two thousand feet into the depths of a great hollow 700 feet below sea level. And there, like a sapphire in a setting of emerald, lies the harp-shaped Sea of Galilee, some thirteen miles long and seven miles wide.

Away to the south stands Mount Tabor, guarding the southern entrance to the basin. Across the lake, brown precipitous slopes riven with deep, treeless gullies, rise to the plateau of Jaulan, or Gaulanitis as it was called in the days of Jesus, the tetrarchy of Philip, son of Herod the Great. Dominating the northern end of the lake beyond the marshes where the Jordan enters, towers the snow-capped bulk of Mount Hermon. And finally, round the north-west end of the lake the hills recede from the water's edge leaving the fertile plain of Gennesaret, whose name, "The garden of abundance,"

Over the hills of Galilee Jesus journeyed with His disciples.
By J. J. TISSOT

suggests its surpassing beauty in the days of Jesus This plain also gave to the sea one of its alternative names, the Lake of Gennesaret.

Today the hills have lost practically all their woods, the lake shore is largely desolate save for a few poor hamlets and scattered bedouin tents, and there is hardly a sail on the blue waters, but as Jesus stood there high up in the hills He saw the whole length of the western shore dotted with splendid cities, backed by rich fields and fruit orchards, and crossed by the thin white lines of great roads converging on the lake from north, west, and south.

From the plateau the modern road twists and turns steeply down past the ruins of a grim black Crusader castle toward the lake, where, on a narrow strip of land between the mountain and the shore stands the town of Tiberias, originally built by Herod Antipas, as his winter capital, a few years before Jesus began His ministry, and which gave to the great sheet of water a third name, the Lake of Tiberias.

The present town looks quite picturesque, with its white domed or flat-roofed houses climbing the hillside and reflected in the calm waters of the lake. But Herod's city, whose scattered ruins lie farther to the south, must have looked far more grand when its marble and gold palace dominated the hillside, surrounded by theatres and other public buildings, and the classical homes of the wealthy courtiers of Herod.

From Herod's capital a road ran southward along the lakeside a mile or so to the thermal springs of Tiberias, which were one of its chief attractions. Around the four warm sulphurous springs are the scattered remains of columns, cornices, and capitals of the baths to which visitors came from all over Palestine, from Syria and Jordan, and even from Rome. Today they still come to the modern Jewish spa built only a few years ago.

It might seem strange that so important a city as Tiberias is never mentioned in the Gospels. The reason is that the population which Herod attracted to it was largely pagan and not Jewish, and though Jesus must more than once have passed through it, He never stopped to preach there, nor did He work there any of His wonderful works.

On their journey from Cana to Capernaum on this occasion Jesus and His companions would certainly not go down into Tiberias, as this was out of their way. Rather would they take the more northerly road which descended the precipitous Valley of Doves to Magdala. In the time of Jesus this lakeside town was important for its dyeing industry, as well as for its market for doves from the wild valley behind, many of which eventually found their way to the temple in Jerusalem as sacrifices. Magdala was also, as we learn later in the Gospel story, the home of Mary Magdalene.

At Magdala the hills recede from the lake and the beautiful plain of Gennesaret begins to open out. Across it Jesus, His family, and the disciples wended their way along the shore road with fertile fields and orchards on one side reaching back to the circle of wooded hills, and the reed-covered strand on the other. Here and there they crossed little tree-lined streams flowing down into the lake or rounded shady oleander-girt bays across which darted kingfishers and other water birds. In the clear, sheltered waters fishing boats at anchor waited for sunset to go out onto the waters of the lake.

Soon they arrived at Bethsaida, or "Fishertown." This was, as the name implies, the home of most of the fishermen at the northern end of the lake. At Capernaum itself there was no satisfactory harbour, but here the contour of the shore formed sheltered bays where the fishing boats could find safe anchorage from the sudden storms which often swept down from the mountains to the north.

As the ruins of Tell Hum, about two miles from where the Jordan pours into the northern end of the lake, have been conclusively identified as Capernaum, Bethsaida must have been located around the beautiful little bay at Tabigha, another two miles farther to the south.

Today, a delightful hospice stands here, amid lovely orchards and gardens, on the shore of the bay, reminding the visitor of the hospitality which awaited Jesus when He came down to the Galilean Sea.

At Bethsaida, Jesus left Andrew, Philip, and John to go to their homes while He, with His family and Peter, went on to Capernaum, to which Peter had moved some time before, perhaps to be near his wife's mother. In one or other of these two homes Jesus, Mary, and His brethren found a warm welcome and hospitality.

What transpired during the few happy days they were together is not recorded, but certainly none realized at the time how largely this lakeside town was to figure in the later ministry of Jesus.

Little did Mary realize that before long her beloved Son would be driven with violence from the village of His boyhood and that Capernaum would become "His town" for the remainder of His earthly days.

Little did Peter think that one day he would be offering his humble dwelling to Jesus as a new home and the centre of His evangelistic labours by the Sea of Galilee. Nor was it in his mind that one day he and his fisher relatives and friends would be giving up their family calling to go out and "catch men" for Jesus. All of this the future was to unfold.

On this occasion Jesus' stay was very brief, "not many days" the Record tells us. Actually, the time of the Passover was drawing on and Jesus had determined that when multitudes would be in Jerusalem from all over Palestine and from the Jewish colonies throughout the Roman Empire, He would go and declare Himself in His "Father's house."

So, when their brief visit was over, Mary returned to Nazareth, and Jesus, with perhaps John and Andrew as His only companions, joined the large caravan setting off down the Great South Road for the feast.

This chapter is based on John 2 :12.

CHAPTER

EIGHTEEN

Cleansing the Temple

JESUS reached Jerusalem some little time before the first Passover of His ministry, in the spring of A.D. 28, and, with His disciples, He erected a temporary booth of branches in some shady grove on the Mount of Olives.

When they went up into the city, the heart of Jesus was saddened by the scene which greeted Him. The Passover was the most important, and by far the busiest feast of the Jewish year, because not only was the Passover commemorated, but it was the time when every faithful Israelite, rich or poor, either sent or brought his annual atonement money of half a shekel to the temple treasury. In consequence, beside the usual market for temple sacrifices and the additional thousands of lambs needed for the Passover meal, many money-changers had to be there to change currencies from all over the Roman Empire into silver half shekels, for no coin with any pagan symbol upon it could go into the temple chests.

All this, of course, was legitimate and necessary business, and no exception could be taken to the money-changers' modest profit of five per cent for the exchange of coins. Unfortunately, however, their greed often tempted them to exact far higher exchange rates, and they further added to their profits by charging heavily for providing change for the purchase of sacrifices, etc. It has been estimated that their takings on the Passover trade was something in the region of seven or eight thousand pounds each year, apart from the vast sums which went into the temple treasury.

The sellers of the Passover lambs and other sacrifices, knowing likewise that the visitors would have to buy from them whatever the cost, also seized the opportunity to make enormous profits.

But that was not the worst. Tempted by the spacious Court of the Gentiles, with its cool and shady colonnades, many of the merchants and bankers had moved out of

---

Jesus drives the merchants and money-changers from the sacred precincts of the temple.
By CARL BLOCH

85

the congested streets leading to the temple and had invaded the sacred precincts, converting them into a vast market in which the crowds of visitors jostled their way among pens of cattle and sheep, cages of doves, and tables piled with coin of every land. The air was filled with the lowing of the cattle, the bleating of sheep, and the hubbub of bargaining as the sellers and exchangers made the most of the days before the feast.

All this, of course, would not have been possible but for the connivance of the high priest and the controllers of the temple who attracted into their own pockets a considerable proportion of the profits from the heavy rentals which they charged. It was not without reason, therefore, that the temple market was called the "bazaar of the sons of Annas."

Jesus took in the sickening scene as He threaded His way across the Court of the Gentiles to Solomon's Porch which gave access to the inner sanctuary. As He observed the greedy traders at work His sadness at the desecration of the sacred enclosure turned to moral indignation. Picking up a few pieces of rush and straw lying around, He twisted them into a rough thong, and, before the vendors realized what was happening, He had opened the pens and begun to drive the animals toward the outer gate of the court. The cages of doves He did not throw down lest harm might come to the gentle creatures, but He ordered their owners to remove them at once.

Then, quickly crossing to the covered colonnades where the exchangers had established themselves, He overturned their tables, scattering the piles of coins in all directions. The crowds fell back in amazement at the audacity of the white-robed Galilean. The merchants cowered beside their pens, and the money-changers dared hardly stoop to retrieve their scattered monies.

Finally, turning upon the greedy sellers and exchangers, Jesus cried in a loud voice, "Take these things hence; make not My Father's house an house of merchandise."

At the age of twelve, on His first boyhood visit to the temple, Jesus hinted at His true nature when He said to His parents, "I must be about My Father's business." On His first appearance in Jerusalem during His ministry He openly declared His Messiahship by His fearless purifying of the sacred courts. By this latter act Jesus fulfilled one of the last utterances of the prophet Malachi concerning His advent, "The Lord, whom ye seek, shall suddenly come to His temple, even the Messenger of the covenant."

Well would it have been if the greedy merchants had been forewarned by the prophet's warning, "But who may abide the day of His coming? and who shall stand when He appeareth? for He is like a refiner's fire, and like fuller's soap: and He shall sit as a refiner and purifier of silver: and He shall purify the sons of Levi."

Years later the disciples who witnessed the divine indignation of Jesus at the desecration of His Father's house, remembered the prophetic words of the Psalmist, "The zeal of Thine house hath eaten Me up."

As soon as the discomfited merchants and exchangers had recovered from the shock of Jesus' entry, they demanded of Him, with a show of anger to cover their alarm, "What sign showest Thou unto us, seeing that Thou doest these things?"

By which they meant to say, "What authority have You to wreck our market, seeing that we have the highest ecclesiastical authorization for being here?"

Jesus did not need to give any other sign of His authority than He had already given, and they knew it, for with all the authority of the Sadducees, none dared stand against Him. In His reply, therefore, Jesus exposed the hatred that was already rising against Him, and which He knew would one day hound Him to the cross. "Destroy this temple," He enigmatically said, meaning His body, "and in three days I will raise it up."

The Jews, thinking that He was referring to the temple buildings, derisively cried, "Forty and six years was this temple in building"—Herod actually had begun its third reconstruction in 20 B.C., and it was still incomplete—"and wilt Thou rear it up in three days?"

Jesus did not correct the Jews' misunderstanding of His words, but John, who was present, remembered it, and after the death and resurrection of Jesus he recalled it to the disciples; and their faith in Him was deepened by the accuracy with which His word was fulfilled.

News of the cleansing of the temple by Jesus spread like wildfire among the thousands in Jerusalem and quickly He acquired a great following among the common people, who resented the extortion and profiteering and regarded Jesus as a champion of their cause. In the succeeding days this following was increased by the many miracles, probably of healing, which He performed, but of which no record has been left for us.

Yet Jesus was not deceived by this initial popularity. He knew that the great majority were interested not so much in His teachings, as in the continuance of the revolutionary work which He had begun in the temple, and which they hoped might soon be directed to cleansing the land of the Roman tyrants. So we read that "Jesus did not commit Himself unto them, because He knew all men, and needed not that any should testify of man: for He knew what was in man." He knew that when their material hopes were not immediately realized they would "walk no more with Him."

The cleansing of the temple was a necessary introduction to His ministry, to expose the apostasy of the religious leaders of His day and to manifest Himself as the true "Messenger of the Covenant." But this did not mean that the kingdom of God was to be established by physical violence. Rather was it to come by a spiritual rebirth in the hearts of men through the mighty working of the Spirit of God, as Jesus clearly explained to the distinguished teacher Nicodemus in the one recorded interview, during this visit to Jerusalem, which has been preserved for us in the Gospel story.

This chapter is based on John 2:13-25.

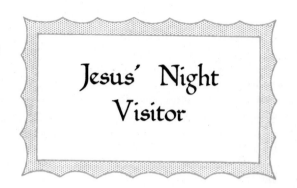

Jesus' Night
Visitor

THE Pharisees had watched the discomfiture of the temple traders with not a little, satisfaction. They themselves frowned upon the laxity of the administrators of the temple and were as appalled by its desecration as was Jesus, though they had not the courage to oppose the powerful Sadducean high priest and his party.

At the same time, the Pharisees could hardly make common cause with Jesus, because His forerunner, John, had humiliated them in the eyes of the people by his caustic remarks about their attention to the minutiæ of form and ceremony, but lack of practical godliness.

There was, therefore, a considerable division of opinion among them about Jesus. Some condemned Him for unauthorized interference in ecclesiastical affairs, while others recognized in His message the authentic prophetic ring, and they did not want to incur the fate of those who, in times past, had "mocked the messengers of God, and despised His words, and misused His prophets, until the wrath of the Lord arose against His people."

One of these latter, a highly respected member of the Sanhedrin, Nicodemus by name, determined to talk with Jesus to see if His zeal could be aligned with those among the Pharisees who recognized the need for reform.

Not wishing, however, to lose dignity by prematurely revealing his sympathy with Jesus, Nicodemus made inquiries as to where Jesus retired each evening, and after nightfall he sought Him out.

"Rabbi," he began, after introducing himself, "we know that Thou art a teacher come from God: for no man can do these miracles that Thou doest, except God be with Him." He and his Pharisee friends would not go so far yet as to recognize His

Jesus reveals to His night visitor, Nicodemus, the way of salvation.
By AXEL HOU

claim to be the Messiah, but as to the source of His prophetic utterance they were in no doubt.

Reading the mind of Nicodemus, and recognizing that all this was introductory to his proposing an alliance with the reformers among the Pharisees, Jesus passed over the compliment and diverted the conversation to the fundamentals of religious experience which were sadly neglected by this prominent party in Jewry.

"Verily, verily, I say unto thee," He admonished Nicodemus, "Except a man be born from above, he cannot see the kingdom of God."

"You Pharisees," He said in effect, "frown upon the worldliness of the Sadducees, and you rejoiced to see Me condemn their lack of reverence for the house of God. But you are really no better than they, for by your multiplication of ceremonial acts, you have obscured true spiritual values. You will all have to experience, Pharisee or Sadducee, a spiritual rebirth if you are to qualify for entrance into the kingdom of God."

Nicodemus was taken aback by this entirely unexpected turn to their discussion. He had hoped to win Jesus' support for a policy of reform within the existing ecclesiastical order, but here was the Galilean Teacher laying the axe at the root of the whole system which he represented.

"But," Nicodemus expostulated, "how can a man be born when he is old? Can he enter the second time into his mother's womb, and be born?"

In any case, why should an Israelite, of the seed of Abraham, and the chosen of God, need a rebirth? He could understand a Gentile being reborn into the faith of Israel. This was indeed a commonly-used analogy, but this experience was not needed by an Israelite, and certainly not by a zealous Pharisee!

Nevertheless, Jesus answered, "Verily, verily, I say unto thee, Except a man be born of water [the symbolic baptism of John] and of the Spirit, he cannot enter into the kingdom of God."

There were many in Israel who were born only "of the flesh." They claimed to be children of Abraham; they exulted in the possession of the oracles of God and the heritage to which they were heirs. But to be "born of the flesh," even the flesh of Israel, was not enough. The essential condition for entrance into the spiritual kingdom of God, was to be "born of the Spirit."

"Marvel not," therefore, Jesus repeated, "that I said unto thee, Ye must be born from above."

"The wind," He went on by way of further explanation, "bloweth where it listeth, and thou hearest the sound thereof, but canst not tell whence it cometh, and whither it goeth: so is everyone that is born of the Spirit." It is not the visible circumstances of birth or environment, however auspicious, which qualify a man for the favour of God. The people of God's choice are those whose natural, sinful hearts have been cleansed and revivified by the unseen winds of the Spirit of God.

Still perplexed to think that there could be any possibility of the ultimate rejection of God's ancient people, Nicodemus shook his head, saying, "How can these things be?"

"Art thou a master of Israel, and knowest not these things?" said Jesus in tones of gentle reprimand. "If I have told you earthly things," the elementary truths of spiritual life, "and ye believe not, how shall ye believe, if I tell you of heavenly things," or the more profound truths of God's eternal purpose?

Still patient with Nicodemus, Jesus called to his remembrance a significant incident during Israel's journey through the wilderness. When they were dying of the deadly bite of the serpents, sent among them as a judgment for sin, they were commanded to look to the symbolic form of a serpent uplifted by Moses in the midst of the camp. In that dire extremity they were saved not by their meticulous attention to the ceremonial acts of the sanctuary services, proper as these were, but by looking to the Saviour whom they foreshadowed.

Soon that symbol in the wilderness was to meet its antitype in the uplifting of God's only-begotten Son upon a cross, and then, no matter how meticulously men continued to comply with form and ceremony, they would be saved from the fatal sting of the serpent of sin only as they looked to and received new life from the upraised Son of God.

"For," said Jesus, "God so loved the world that He gave His only begotten Son, that whosoever believeth in Him, should not perish, but have everlasting life."

So, Jesus explained to the amazed Nicodemus, whether one is a Sadducee or a Pharisee, signifies nothing. Whether one is an Israelite according to the flesh or a Gentile, does not matter. What only matters is that "he that believeth on Him is not condemned: but he that believeth not is condemned already" by his refusal of the gift of grace.

That only a remnant of Israel after the flesh, and indeed of the world as a whole, would make the right choice, Jesus sadly indicated as He concluded, "And this is the condemnation, that light is come into the world, and men loved darkness rather than light, because their deeds were evil."

As Nicodemus left Jesus and took the dark road over the Kidron river and up into Jerusalem again, he knew that he himself was turning from the "light" and going back into the "darkness" of a dead ecclesiasticism. In his heart he longed to follow Jesus, but for three long years he could not bring himself to make the great decision. The impression of that momentous interview, however, never left him. Time and again he did what he could to restrain the Sanhedrin from violent action against Jesus, but when, on the fatal day of the crucifixion, he saw Jesus "uplifted" on the cross, he remembered what Jesus had foretold and the moment of supreme tragedy for the disciples was the moment of conviction for him. He made his decision and was born again "from above."

There are many today, like Nicodemus, who have heard the call of Christ, but who cannot bring themselves openly to forsake all to follow Him. Oh, that they might learn from his experience and, before it is for ever too late, come forth out of the darkness, whether of unbelief or of error, into light and life in Him.

This chapter is based on John 3:1-21.

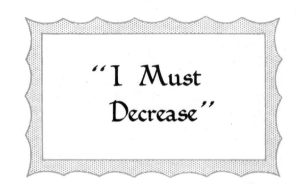

"I Must Decrease"

THE prophet Isaiah, centuries before Jesus came, declared that the Messiah would not be "received" by His own, and Jesus' first visit to Jerusalem after the beginning of His ministry confirmed this.

The Sadducees were furious with Him for condemning their lucrative trade in the temple courts. The Pharisees, apart from a few like Nicodemus, were equally hostile. He had achieved some popularity with the common people, but Jesus knew that their interest was in the material benefits accruing from His miracles rather than in the message He bore.

So, soon after the feast of the Passover was over, He left the capital and descended into the Jordan valley where John was still preaching and baptizing.

Not wishing to interrupt this closing phase of John's ministry, Jesus did not go near Aenon, where John was located, but moved to the northern end of the valley, probably not far from the entrance to the Wady Farah which runs up into Samaria, for this was the way He took some months later when He returned to Galilee.

If Jesus hoped for a time of quiet communion with His disciples, He must have been disappointed, for, when the people discovered where He had gone, multitudes followed Him, until soon He had a congregation greater even than had gone out to hear the Baptist. Ever ready to minister, Jesus began to teach, and His disciples, most likely John and Andrew, baptized those who responded to His call, "Repent, for the kingdom of heaven is at hand."

When John's disciples heard of the success of Jesus' ministry in northern Judea, they were jealous and expressed their resentment. But the Baptist would allow no exaltation of his ministry at the expense of Christ's. "A man," he said to his aggrieved disciples, "can receive nothing, except it be given him from heaven. Ye yourselves

There was no jealousy in John's heart that Jesus was displacing him in the affections of the people.
By J. J. TISSOT

bear me witness that I said, I am not the Christ, but that I am sent before Him."

To help them to see the relationship between Jesus and himself, John used a striking and beautiful illustration. Jesus, he said, is the "Bridegroom," and it is natural that the "bride," that is His followers, should be attracted to Him. He, John, occupied the position of the "friend" of the Bridegroom who, like the professional go-between in eastern marriages, had been instrumental in introducing Jesus to the people. Now that the union was being realized, his work was ending and he was ready to stand back, rejoicing as he saw the joy of the bride in the company of the Bridegroom. In this, he declared, "my joy . . . is fulfilled."

Then, in almost his last recorded words, John revealed the true greatness of his character. "He must increase," he said, "but I must decrease." There was no tinge of jealousy in John's humble heart that Jesus had displaced him in the affections of the people. He knew he had done the work which God sent him to do. And now that the One whom he was deputed to announce had come, he was ready and happy to step aside. What an example of selfless service to every worker for God!

Whether the remaining verses in the third chapter of John's gospel are a further explanation by the Baptist to his disciples, or the inspired comment of the apostle, it is difficult to decide, but to whomsoever they should be credited, they vividly set forth the fundamental difference between John and Jesus.

John was "sent from God," but in his origin he was "of the earth," a man chosen from among men. Jesus, on the other hand, "came down from above." He was God incarnate.

There was "none born of woman" greater than John, as Jesus said on a later occasion, but Jesus Himself, was apart from and "above" all men.

The testimony of John was likewise "of the earth;" he knew only "in part." Jesus, by contrast, testified of what He had "seen and heard" in the courts of heaven and in the very presence of God.

John gave an inspired testimony to the Coming One, but "He whom God hath sent" spoke the very "words of God."

John had received of the "spirit and power of Elijah" for the fulfilment of his task, but to Jesus, God had given the Spirit without "measure" or restriction.

John witnessed to the power of God, but the Father gave "all power" into the hand of the Son.

The work of John was to announce the saving efficacy of Christ, but the Son had life in Himself. "He that believeth on the Son hath everlasting life," and conversely, "He that believeth not the Son, shall not see life."

These were the reasons why the faithful yet preparatory ministry of John was coming to its end, and why John had to "decrease" in order that the work of Jesus might "increase" to its glorious consummation.

After his work of introduction had been successfully completed, the "friend" of the bridegroom was usually able to enjoy the reward of his faithful efforts, but the analogy in the case of John did not extend to this. Sad to say, no such tranquil end was to be his.

As the greater part of John's ministry was in Perea, on the other side of the River Jordan, it was to be expected that he would come to the notice of Herod Antipas, tetrarch of Galilee and Perea. So curious, in fact, was Herod about John's message that more than once he summoned him into his presence to question him. And brutal and voluptuous as Antipas was, like all the Herods, he recognized John as "a just man and an holy." But there was one matter about which John spoke which worried Herod and infuriated his wife Herodias. "It is not lawful," John fearlessly said, "for thee to have thy brother's wife."

It was indeed a sordid story. Herod had been married to the daughter of Aretas, the Nabatean king of Petra, whose realm lay immediately to the south of Perea in what was once ancient Edom. While on a visit to Rome, however, he became enamoured of Herodias, the wife of his half-brother Philip, who had been disinherited by Herod the Great and was living in a private capacity there. Philip's wife was an unscrupulous and ambitious woman who despised her husband because he was the only Herod without a tetrarchy. So seizing her opportunity, she persuaded Antipas to divorce the daughter of Aretas and marry her.

Besides being an act of treachery toward Philip, and an adulterous association while he still lived, it was also an unlawful union, for Herodias was already both the sister-in-law and niece of Herod.

News of the plot reached the wife of Antipas before his return, whereupon she promptly fled from the court to her father. The way was thus cleared for the consummation of the evil match, and Herodias was installed as Herod's wife.

When John pointed out to Herod his terrible sin, which was an offence to God and a scandal to his people, Herodias saw that her husband was deeply affected, and, fearing that he might send her back to Philip, she demanded that John should be punished with death for his insult to her. Herod could not bring himself to perpetrate such a crime for he feared John, and he also feared the people, who recognized John as a prophet of God. But to appease Herodias he took John into "protective custody," incarcerating him in the remote castle of Machærus in the wild hills of Moab about six miles east of the Dead Sea.

A Roman road can still be traced up to the castle, the ruins of which are spread over an area of a square mile on the summit of a mountain some 3,700 feet above sea level. Within the walls of the fortress was a sumptuous palace, where Herod stayed when visiting southern Perea, and an impregnable keep or citadel some 500 feet higher, right on the summit of the mountain. In one of its ruined turrets there can still be seen holes in the masonry for the rings to which prisoners' chains were secured.

At the time Herod had no intention of doing any bodily harm to John. When the wrath of Herodias was allayed he doubtless purposed to let him quietly go.

His wife, however, was bitter at heart against the prophet and determined upon his destruction. The opportunity came sooner than she expected and John never again saw the outside of the "Black Fortress" of Machærus.

This chapter is based on John 3:22-36; Matthew 14:3-5; Mark 6:17-20; Luke 3:19, 20.

The Water of Life

FOR some months Jesus preached and His disciples baptized in or near the Jordan Valley, watched by the spies of the Pharisees. Then, toward winter, realizing that their growing hostility might provoke a crisis before the time, He decided to leave Judea and return to His native Galilee.

If He had taken the usual road He would have followed the Jordan Valley as far as Bethshan, and then ascended the Vale of Jezreel. But, says the Record, very significantly, "He must needs go through Samaria."

We may well ask why this was necessary, seeing that on a later occasion Jesus expressly stated that He was not sent "but unto the lost sheep of the house of Israel." The answer is that while the Gospel had first to be offered to Israel before its general extension to the Gentile world, Jesus wished to reveal by "token" acts that He had come to save not one nation, but the whole "world." At this very time, as He was sadly leaving Judea, there were souls in Samaria ready to respond to the Gospel, and so He was impressed by the Spirit to go that way.

From the depths of the Jordan gorge, 1,100 feet below sea level, to the uplands of Samaria was a journey of some twenty miles, involving a climb of around 3,000 feet. The easiest way was along the old Roman Road up the Wady Farah, but as Jesus' first stopping place was at Jacob's Well, it is likely that He and His disciples took the more direct but steeper track due west over the hills. The journey was long and tiring, but a rewarding sight greeted their eyes as they reached the crest of the mountain ridge and began to descend into one of the most fertile plains in all Samaria.

For miles to the east and south stretched green pastures and waving fields of barley and wheat. The modern Arabic name of the district, Mukhna, means "cornfields."

Right ahead of them, standing guard over the Vale of Shechem which wound

---

Jesus offers the Water of Life to the Samaritan woman at Jacob's Well.
By CARL BLOCH

round to Samaria, were the historic mountains Gerizim and Ebal. It was from these slopes that Joshua bade Israel choose between the blessings and the curses of God when they first occupied Canaan.

Down in the centre of the green expanse was Jacob's Well and the parcel of ground that he bought from the children of Hamor, where later the bones of Joseph were buried.

Today the hills and valley are barer, but the view is still beautiful, and Jacob's Well remains one of the best authenticated sacred sites in the land. In the time of Jesus it stood in the open fields with only a shelter of branches to protect its mouth. Now it is in the vaulted crypt of a church built around it on the foundations of earlier churches going back to the first centuries of the Christian era.

Once the well was over 100 feet deep. Now rubbish has reduced its depth to about seventy, but it still contains water which is dispensed to visitors in little bottles by an attendant priest.

About 200 yards north of the well is the traditional tomb of Joseph. The present building is a typical Moslem wely, or holy man's grave, for Joseph is revered by Mohammedans as well as Jews and Christians, but the site itself may be ancient.

What memories must have crowded into the mind of Jesus as He looked down upon the lovely scene! What changes had taken place in the valley since Jacob dug his well 1,500 years before!

Over the mountains from the Jordan, Joshua led the armies of Israel here in their first victorious thrust, and eventually the tribes of Ephraim and Manasseh were settled to the south and north.

When the ten tribes separated themselves from Judah, Samaria became the heart of the kingdom of Israel and its capital the centre of idolatrous calf worship under Jeroboam and his successors.

When their iniquity came to the full and the northern kingdom was given into the hands of the Assyrians, King Sargon carried multitudes of Israelites away captive, while heathen peoples from the east were settled by his successor, Esarhaddon, among the remnant which was not deported. Intermarriage took place, and the religion of the Samaritans, as the mixed people came to be called, was further corrupted by the idolatrous practices introduced by the colonists.

After the return of the Jews from their Babylonian captivity, an attempt was made by the Samaritans to claim kinship with them, but their help in the building of the temple was refused. In reply, a Samaritan temple was built on Mount Gerizim, and Manasseh, the runaway brother of the high priest in Jerusalem, who had married a daughter of Sanballat, was made high priest of the Samaritans.

The five books of Moses were adopted as the authoritative revelation of God, but all the later books, exalting Jerusalem, were rejected. The claim was even advanced that Moriah, the place of Abraham's sacrifice, was Gerizim and not Zion! In the Gerizim temple the Mosaic services were carried on and Jacob and Joseph were revered as the forefathers of the Samaritans.

As the centuries passed by, the Jews and Samaritans moved farther and farther apart, and during the Maccabean wars the Jewish zealots under John Hyrcanus destroyed the temple on Gerizim as a punishment for their apostasy.

By the time Jesus was born, the whole of Palestine had been reunited again under Herod the Great, and when He began His ministry, Judea and Samaria was a Roman province. Though open hostility was no longer possible under the eye of the Roman procurator, the prejudice continued, and the more orthodox Jews, when journeying to Galilee, would go right round Samaria rather than set foot upon its soil.

The Galileans, in general, did not carry their prejudice against the Samaritans as far as the Jews of the south, and the disciples doubtless did not take any exception to the decision of Jesus to go through Samaria, but little did they anticipate what was to happen on the way.

It was the "sixth hour," or about noon, when Jesus and His disciples reached Jacob's Well. As Jesus sat down to rest on the parapet of the well, the disciples proposed that they should go into the village of Sychar to buy food. This village, the modern Askar, was half a mile away on the slope of Mount Ebal.

No sooner had the disciples gone than a woman came down the road, a water pot on her head, to draw water at the well. It may seem strange that she should walk so far when there were abundant springs in Sychar. It may be, however, that, being a woman of questionable repute, she preferred to go there rather than to the more frequented well in the village, and at this hour rather than in the early morning or near sunset.

Judging by His dress that Jesus was a Jew, she did not speak. She lowered her pitcher by a long cord into the well, drew it up brimming full, and was about to lift it to her head and depart when Jesus, in kindly tones, requested a drink.

She swung round in surprise that He should speak to a Samaritan, and to a woman at that, for the strict Jew would not even acknowledge his daughter, his sister, or his wife in public! "How is it that Thou, being a Jew, askest drink of me, which am a woman of Samaria?" she demanded.

But Jesus was not to be drawn into a discussion on national prejudice. Beyond His bodily need to quench His thirst, the motive of Jesus in speaking with her was to bring her a spiritual blessing. So He replied: "If thou knewest the gift of God, and who it is that saith to thee, Give Me to drink; thou wouldst have asked of Him, and He would have given thee living water." He could have chosen no more appropriate a description of His teaching. Water is one of the most vital of man's physical needs and in lands like Palestine, where there are long rainless periods, it is sought after and conserved as the veritable water of life. The prime need of the spirit of man is likewise "living water" from the ever-fresh and never-failing "wells of salvation." "With Thee," declared the Psalmist to God, "is the fountain of life." And for it his soul longed as "in a dry and thirsty land, where no water is."

Did Jesus recall, as He spoke with the woman of Sychar, the promise to Joseph, whose tomb was but a few yards away? "Joseph is a fruitful bough, even a fruitful bough by a wall; whose branches run over the wall." Certainly He longed that such

OPPOSITE

A girl of modern Bethlehem.

ABOVE

A Christian Arab kneels beside the star marking the traditional birthplace of Jesus in the Cave of the Nativity, Bethlehem.

RIGHT

Across the cave from the Star of Bethlehem is a rock niche which may have been the manger in which Jesus was laid.

an experience might come to this poor woman and many others in this land so full of memories of the patriarchs.

But the woman was mystified by His enigmatical remark. Incredulously she demanded how He could produce water of any kind, seeing that He had neither pitcher nor rope to draw with.

"Whosoever drinketh of the water that I shall give him shall never thirst," Jesus repeated; "but the water that I shall give him shall be in him a well of water springing up into everlasting life."

Still thinking that Jesus was talking of the water from some remarkable spring, she pleaded, "Sir, give me this water, that I thirst not, neither come hither to draw."

Her interest was now aroused and the time had come for Jesus to reveal to the woman her real need. "Go, call thy husband, and come hither," He said to her.

Not suspecting that this chance traveller could know anything of her private life, she replied casually, "I have no husband."

Jesus' next words laid bare the sinful past which had marred her life. "Thou hast well said, I have no husband: for thou hast had five husbands; and he whom thou now hast is not thy husband."

For a moment the woman was taken completely aback by this penetrating exposure. Quickly recovering herself, however, she sought to turn the conversation in a less embarrassing direction.

"I perceive that Thou art a prophet," she countered. "Our fathers worshipped in this mountain," and she pointed to Mount Gerizim, on the top of which, 800 feet above them, the ruins of the Samaritan temple destroyed by John Hyrcanus still stood; "and ye say, that in Jerusalem is the place where men ought to worship."

Allowing the woman, for the moment, her new choice of topic, Jesus answered earnestly, "Ye worship ye know not what: . . . for salvation is of the Jews."

True worship is not a matter of place but of the condition of the heart. "God is a Spirit: and they that worship Him must worship Him in spirit and in truth."

"Believe Me," He added, "the hour cometh, when ye shall neither in this mountain, nor yet at Jerusalem, worship the Father. . . . The hour cometh, and now is, when the true worshippers shall worship the Father in spirit and in truth: for the Father seeketh such to worship Him."

Thinking that the Stranger must be referring to the reformation that would take place when Messiah appeared, for whom the Samaritans looked equally with the Jews, she confessed, "I know that Messiah cometh, which is called Christ: when He is come, He will tell us all things."

Then Jesus declared plainly, "I that speak unto thee am He."

As He made this startling announcement, the disciples arrived back from Sychar. In amazement they looked at their Master, questioning in their hearts that He should talk openly with a strange woman. But the woman seemed not to notice them, so profoundly had she been affected by the words of Jesus. Leaving her water pot where she had placed it when she began to talk with Him, she turned without a word and hurried back along the road the disciples had come. Reaching Sychar she called her neighbours and blurted out, "Come, see a Man, which told me all things that ever I did: is not this the Christ?"

Their curiosity was aroused by the woman's story and the astonishing change which had come over her, and excitedly they set out across the fields to the well.

While the woman was talking with her neighbours the disciples were setting before Jesus the food they had brought. "Master, eat," they urged. Great was their surprise when He replied, "I have meat to eat that ye know not of."

What did He mean? they wondered. Had the woman given Him something? Noticing their questioning among themselves Jesus explained, "My meat is to do the will of Him that sent Me, and to finish His work."

Then pointing across the fields of growing corn He went on, "Say not ye, There are yet four months, and then cometh harvest? behold, I say unto you, Lift up your eyes, and look on the fields; for they are white already to harvest." And as they looked in the direction that Jesus indicated, they saw a crowd of Samaritans from Sychar hurrying toward the well.

This was the reason why Jesus had to come through Samaria. Though the disciples had not realized it, a harvest of souls awaited His reaping hands.

Beautifully Jesus then portrayed to His disciples the reward of the work of spiritual husbandry in which they were soon to engage. "He that reapeth receiveth wages, and gathereth fruit unto life eternal: that both he that soweth and he that reapeth may rejoice together."

By now the Samaritans were crowding round, and though a little while before Jesus had been hungry, thirsty, and tired, He was revived by the call to minister, and dispensed to them the "Bread of life" and the "Living water." So eager was their response that they pleaded with Jesus to stay among them.

At the end of two days, as Jesus prepared to depart, the Samaritan believers confessed their personal faith in Him. "Now we believe," they declared to the woman who had introduced them to Jesus, "not because of thy saying: for we have heard Him ourselves, and know that this is indeed the Christ, the Saviour of the world."

No more wonderful testimony concerning Jesus had yet been heard, and remarkably enough, those who bore it were not Jews, but "aliens from the commonwealth of Israel." Already it was becoming clear that while His own people would "receive Him not," souls in the most unexpected places would find salvation through Him. The harvest in Samaria was a foretaste of the triumphs of the Gospel to the earth's far ends.

This chapter is based on John 4:1-42.

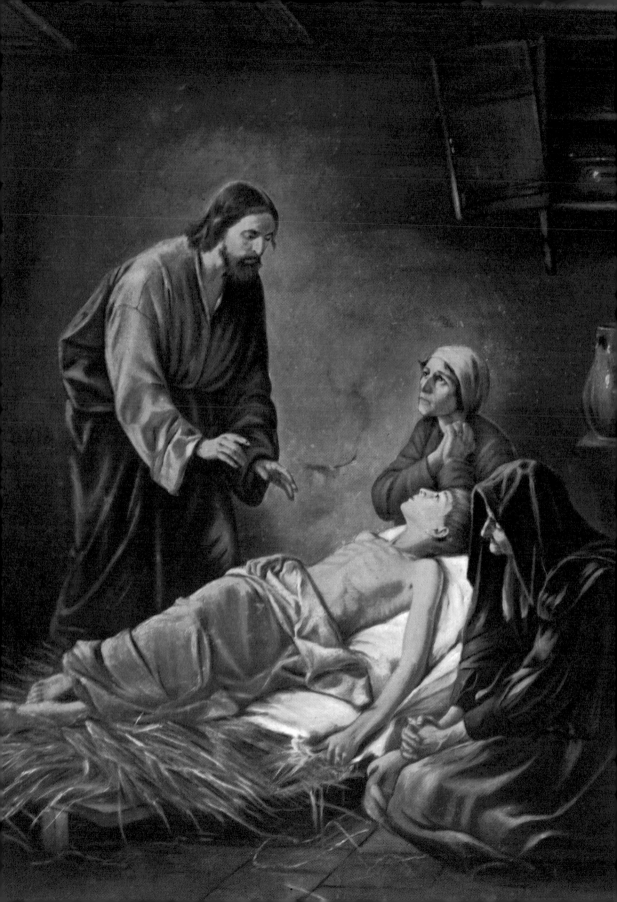

Interlude in Galilee

I F Jesus had been looking for ease and popularity in His ministry He might well have stayed among the open-minded and responsive Samaritans. But Jesus knew that the opportunity of the Gospel had to be extended to the "house of Israel" before it should go to "Samaria" and to "the uttermost part of the earth."

So, after only two days' stay at Sychar, Jesus set off with His disciples up the green valley of Shechem and past ancient Samaria. In those days it was a fine city, beautified shortly before by Herod the Great, and called Sebaste, which was the Greek equivalent of the Latin title Augustus, in honour of the Roman Emperor. Today little of it remains, but on the highest levels of the mound is the monumental staircase of the temple erected by Herod to Augustus. The colossal statue of Augustus which once stood in front of it was found by the modern excavators lying fallen at the bottom of the staircase. When Jesus passed that way the temple stood in all its pagan glory, as also did the vast hippodrome to the north of the town, of which also only a few column bases now remain.

Across the plain of Dothan, Jesus and His companions continued their way to En-gannim, where they left Samaria behind and entered Galilee. One might have expected that Jesus would make straight for Nazareth where His mother and His brothers and sisters still lived. But Jesus had a premonition of what His reception would be in His home town. "A prophet," He knew from the past experience of God's messengers, "hath no honour in his own country." So, travelling unobtrusively, He passed by Nazareth and came to Cana where He had turned water into wine at the wedding feast. Just where He stayed we are not told, but this family would certainly have been glad to offer Him hospitality. Or He may have lodged at the home of His new-found disciple, Nathanael, whose home was there.

Jesus went about all Galilee relieving the suffering and distressed. Today He is still the "Great Physician."

By ZIMMERMANN

His return was hailed with delight by the Galileans, and crowds came to Cana to meet Him. Many of these Galileans had been at the feast of the Passover the previous spring and, if they had not seen the cleansing of the temple by Jesus, they had heard of His courageous act, and were proud to think that one of their fellow countrymen had exposed the abuses in the capital.

There were others who had heard of the miracles Jesus had wrought in Judea and hastened to Him for help and healing. One of these was a certain Jewish nobleman of Capernaum whose son was grievously sick from a fever common by the lakeside. The man's name is not recorded, but, from a later reference by Luke, it may well have been Chuza, a steward or revenue officer in the service of Herod Antipas, tetrarch of Galilee and Perea.

As soon as he heard that Jesus was as near as Cana, this court official determined to go in person to seek His aid. The distance from Capernaum was about sixteen miles and it was about one o'clock in the afternoon before he got there. Wasting no time, he found Jesus and begged Him to come quickly and save his son.

From the manner of the nobleman's request Jesus realized that the man was indifferent as to who Jesus was or what message He preached; he was concerned only that His healing power should be exercised on behalf of his son. But Jesus could not permit the nobleman to regard Him merely as an itinerant healer and so, not giving any indication as to whether or not He would respond to the request, He replied, "Except ye see signs and wonders, ye will not believe." "If I work some wonder among you," He said in effect, "you will be prepared to consider My message. But if only you would believe on Me the blessings you seek, and more, would be added to you."

The import of Jesus' words went home to the nobleman's heart and a fear came over him that his selfish approach might cost him his son's life. In desperation he pleaded, "Sir, come down ere my child die."

To the cry of the agonized heart Jesus was never unresponsive, and He kept the nobleman in suspense no longer. "Go thy way," He said gently: "thy son liveth."

The nobleman's taut nerves relaxed and a calm overspread his anxious face. He felt the power in the quiet words of Jesus and he knew that it was all right with his child. In that moment he "believed," not merely in the assurance that Jesus gave him, but in Jesus Himself.

So confident was the nobleman that all would be well when he got back home, that he did not attempt the return journey that night. Instead he enjoyed the first night's rest he had had for a long time. The next morning early he was on his way. As he neared Capernaum in the early afternoon he saw his servants coming along the road to meet him. On reaching them, he asked how his son was and learned, just as he expected, that the fever had completely gone.

What time was it that the turn in his condition came? he asked them, and they replied, "Yesterday at the seventh hour the fever left him." And the nobleman knew that at the very hour that Jesus had spoken with him, his son was healed.

With thankful heart he hurried home and told his wife, their beloved boy, and all in the house of his interview with Jesus, and of the faith that had been awakened in his heart. And all his house "believed" with him and were numbered among the disciples of Jesus.

Nor is that the end of the story of the second miracle which Jesus wrought in Cana of Galilee. For if the nobleman was indeed Chuza, Herod's steward, it was his wife, Joanna, who later ministered to Jesus of her "substance" to help Him in His work.

This chapter is based on John 4:43-54.

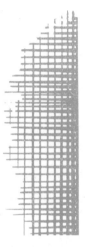

Many who had heard of the miracles Jesus did in Judea hurried to Him for help and healing.

By J. HOFMANN

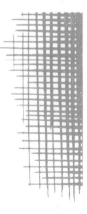

CHAPTER TWENTY-THREE

At the Pool
of Bethesda

OF Jesus' labours in Galilee during the winter of A.D. 28, after the second miracle at Cana, we know nothing. His disciples seemingly returned to their boats on Galilee, while He lived in comparative seclusion in Cana or Capernaum, awaiting the next Passover, when the final issue of His Judean ministry would be decided. Not until "the feast of the Jews" drew near does the curtain lift, and we see Jesus setting off again for the capital.

Jesus knew that His cleansing of the temple the previous year had aroused the bitter enmity of the rulers of the Jews, and that His ministry by the Jordan, parallel with that of John, had intensified their opposition. They had already "delivered up" John at the instigation of Herodias, and Jesus knew that the priests were seeking an occasion to denounce Him also. Yet He desired to give them one more chance to receive Him. He would go again, and in the plainest terms declare Himself and His mission. If they "received Him not," they would be left without excuse.

There is no mention of any of His disciples accompanying Him on this occasion, for as yet none had been formally called into His service. The fact, however, that John records this momentous visit, as also the events of His previous journey to Jerusalem, suggests that he had already become a close companion of Jesus, though, with his customary modesty, he does not intrude himself into the story.

Soon after the arrival of Jesus in Jerusalem, He was walking on the Sabbath by the Pool of Bethesda, which lay to the north of the temple area, close by the Sheep Gate, now called St. Stephen's Gate from the tradition that the first Christian martyr was later dragged through it to his death.

Those who have tried to reconstruct the Jerusalem of the first century, have made various suggestions as to the site of this pool, and for a long time it was identified

with a filled-in reservoir called Birket Israel which abuts onto the north wall of
the temple. Toward the end of the last century, however, there was discovered beneath
the courtyard of the medieval Church of St. Anne on the other side of the road
leading to the Sheep Gate, a hitherto unknown pool, the remains of which correspond
exactly in position and form with the Bible description of Bethesda.

Originally it comprised two basins, each some forty-three yards square, with
pillared porticos running along the four sides and with a fifth between the pools.
These were the "five porches" mentioned in the Bible account.

Around Jerusalem there are a number of intermittent springs resulting from some
peculiar conformation of the subterranean channels in the limestone mass upon which
Jerusalem is built, and evidently one of these fed the Pool of Bethesda. At certain
intervals a surge of water would pour into the pool, "troubling" the water. After a
short period the level would subside and the water would remain quiet until the
next surge. The idea that the troubling was caused by the descent of an angel is not
biblical. It is not found in the earliest manuscripts of the New Testament and is
therefore justifiably omitted from the Revised Version. It is a copyist's attempted
explanation which somehow was allowed to creep into the text.

The waters of the spring seem to have been highly impregnated with mineral
matter—Jerome in later days mentions their reddish colour—which consequently
would have a curative value in certain physical conditions, and the fame of these
healing properties had given to the pool the name Bethesda, which means "House
of Mercy."

It was believed that at the time of the troubling, the waters had specially marked
healing virtues, and so the porticos were always thronged by sick people waiting
to descend quickly into the pool.

It was just about the time a "troubling" was expected, that Jesus went in among
the multitude of sufferers. As He gazed with infinite pity upon them, one particular
man, the most abject of them all, caught His eye. In his dissolute youth this man had
contracted a disease which had withered his limbs and left him paralysed.

Thirty-eight years he had been afflicted, and for many of them he had frequented
the pool hoping that someone would help him down into it during the "troubling."
But everyone there was either trying to get down himself or was assisting a friend,
and no-one had ever offered him aid. Now he came as a matter of habit, but without
hope. The heart of Jesus went out to the poor man in his friendlessness and, stooping
down, He said quietly, "Wilt thou be made whole?"

A momentary hope stirred in the breast of the paralytic as he looked into the
face of his sympathetic questioner. Then sinking back in despairing resignation, he
replied, "Sir, I have no man, when the water is troubled, to put me into the pool."

He had turned away disconsolately to stare at the pool when Jesus spoke again.
"Rise, take up thy bed [or sleeping mat], and walk." As the astounding words fell
on his ears a tingling of life passed through his withered limbs. The ertswhile dead
muscles tautened, and hardly realizing what he was doing, he made to obey the
command, and in a moment he was on his feet.

Grasping his mat and blanket he turned to thank his Benefactor, but Jesus had already disappeared among the crowd which quickly gathered.

The news of the miracle brought some of the Jewish rabbis hurrying to the scene. As they came up they met the man with his sleeping mat on his shoulder, walking down the street. Forgetting the wonderful act of healing which had taken place they were scandalized at this flagrant breach of the rabbinical ordinances. "It is the Sabbath day," they cried, advancing menacingly toward him: "It is not lawful for thee to carry thy bed."

The attitude of the Pharisees was indicative of the spiritless ritualism which had come over the Jewish religion in the days of Jesus. Sabbath-keeping, as indeed every other act of worship, had entirely lost its spiritual significance and had become a mere conformity to a host of petty rules. On the Sabbath, for example, help might be given to the sick only if life was in danger. If there was no serious emergency they must wait to be treated until after the Sabbath. As the paralytic was in no danger of dying, Jesus had contravened their legalistic interpretation of "work."

Again, they took the divine admonition that no burden should be borne on the Sabbath, to fantastic lengths. A pin upon a garment was a burden not to be borne. To carry a loaf of bread was equally illegal. And to be seen carrying a sleeping mat and blanket on Sabbath was infamous!

When the Pharisees met the restored paralytic, therefore, their indignation was aroused on two counts, first that an act of healing should have been performed unnecessarily during the Sabbath hours, and secondly because in no circumstances should the man have carried his bed on Sabbath, particularly in the open streets.

The healed man was taken aback by this public rebuff and could only blurt out, "He that made me whole, the same said unto me, Take up thy bed, and walk."

His reply angered the Pharisees the more. Their authority was not to be sidetracked by the man disowning responsibility for his action. So they demanded, "What man is that which said unto thee, Take up thy bed, and walk?" How dare anyone defy the Sabbath ordinances, and encourage another to break them?

But the man could not say who his Benefactor was. He only saw Him during their brief conversation and as soon as He had accomplished the miracle, He had gone.

The Jewish rulers, however, need not have asked, for they knew only one Man who could have performed such a miracle. Jesus must be back in Jerusalem. Peremptorily they dismissed the man and conferred among themselves how they might accuse the Galilean and curb His growing influence among the people.

Having taken his bed home, the restored paralytic made his way to the temple to offer thanks to God for his healing, and also to tell his wonderful story among the crowds of worshippers.

As he crossed one of the courts he suddenly came face to face with Jesus. Immediately he began to express his gratitude. Kindly, but solemnly, Jesus said to him, "Behold, thou art made whole: sin no more, lest a worse thing come unto thee." Every miracle of healing which Jesus performed was intended as a prelude to the spiritual restoration of the sufferer, and Jesus wanted this man to realize that his cure would not be complete if it did not lead to sincere repentance for sin, and a determination henceforth to live a life pleasing to God.

As Jesus passed on His way the man remembered that he had not been able to identify Jesus to the priests, and wishing to show them that their anger was uncalled for he hurried off to find them again. But his hopes of allaying their wrath were speedily disappointed. As soon as he confirmed their fears that the alleged Sabbath-breaker was none other than the Galilean who had humiliated them at the previous Passover, their rage knew no bounds. This miracle performed on the Sabbath was an open challenge to their authority. He must be officially reprimanded and if He would not recant He must be stopped, if necessary, by force.

Little did they realize as they dispatched messengers to find Jesus and summon Him for questioning before the Sanhedrin, the dire consequences to themselves and the nation of their blindness and unbelief.

This chapter is based on John 5 :1-15.

"Wilt thou be made whole?" Jesus asked the poor cripple at Bethesda.
By CARL BLOCH

CHAPTER TWENTY-FOUR

What Think Ye of Christ?

WHEN the messengers from the Jewish rulers found Jesus and summoned Him to their presence, He was very ready to accompany them. This was indeed the opportunity for which He had been waiting, and which He had intended His Sabbath miracle at Bethesda to precipitate.

The leaders of the nation were now to be plainly confronted with the claims of His Person and mission, and they would have to decide once and for all whether they would "receive" Him or no. If they persisted in rejecting Him, then their unbelief would be starkly manifest, and their condemnation complete.

In Jesus' day there were three Sanhedrins. The Small Sanhedrin, comprising twenty-three members, met in a chamber near the Shushan or Golden Gate in the Great Court of the Temple. The Court of Appeal was housed near the Nicanor Gate in the Court of the Priests. The Great Sanhedrin, the highest ecclesiastical body among the Jews, met originally in the House of Hewn Stones in the Court of the Israelites, but by this time it may have moved to a new location outside the temple area.

Whether Jesus was summoned before any specific body of priests, or before such as could quickly be called together, we do not know. But certainly it was a representative group of the highest ecclesiastical officers who gathered to rebuke Jesus and warn Him of the danger of continuing to flout their authority.

Jesus began His defence by decisively refuting the charge of Sabbath-breaking they brought against Him. True, the Sabbath was a day when the toil of the week should cease and when burdens should be laid down in order that master and servant might equally enjoy physical relaxation and spiritual refreshment. But that did not mean that the Sabbath was to be a day of mere inactivity. In a very real sense, Jesus declared, "My Father worketh hitherto, and I work," on the Sabbath day.

The most important question in the world is, "What think ye of Christ?" for the answer will determine our eternal destiny.   By AUGUST JERNDORFF

God's beneficence does not cease each Sabbath as darkness falls. The sun rises and Nature continues to yield her bounties on the Sabbath. God does not, therefore, contradict Himself by continuing His works of providence and redemption on His holy day. The healing of the paralytic was a merciful act of God, as much as it was an act of Jesus, for the power to heal was given Him of His Father, and so, in condemning Him, they were condemning God Himself. Works of human necessity and of mercy were in line with God's own activity on every Sabbath day, and, therefore, as Jesus said on a later occasion, it is "lawful to do good on the Sabbath day."

Stung to new fury by Jesus' rebuttal of their charge of Sabbath-breaking, the rabbis seized upon His reference to His Father in order to pin upon Him the even more serious charge of blasphemy. "He not only had broken the Sabbath," they declared, "but said also that God was His Father, making Himself equal with God."

But this was the precise issue which Jesus intended His accusers to face. Plainly and explicitly, therefore, He repeated His claim that He was the very Son of God and that His Father was completely identified with Him in His every word and action.

"The Son," He asserted, "can do nothing of Himself, but what He seeth the Father do," and "what things soever He [the Father] doeth, these also doeth the Son likewise. For the Father loveth the Son, and showeth Him all things that He Himself doeth."

What they had seen, moreover, was but the beginning of the things which His Father and He would do. Yet "greater works than these" would they see, even to the supreme act of omnipotence, the raising of the dead. "For as the Father raiseth up the dead, and quickeneth them; even so the Son quickeneth whom He will."

There was something else, too, which His accusers should understand. Far from their being His judges and His life lying in their hands, He had received of His Father the power of life and death for every living soul. For the Father had determined not to judge apart from the Son, but had "committed all judgment unto the Son."

"Verily, verily, I say unto you," Jesus solemnly declared, "He that heareth My word, and believeth on Him that sent Me, hath everlasting life, and shall not come into condemnation." Even though such ones might fall asleep in physical death "the hour is coming," He said, "when the dead shall hear the voice of the Son of God," and they that hear shall live again.

Over those, however, who would not hear His word and believe in Him, Jesus continued, the Father had "given Him authority to execute judgment, . . . because He is the Son of man."

"Marvel not at this," therefore, said Jesus in solemn tones: "for the hour is coming, in the which all that are in the graves shall hear His voice, and shall come forth; they that have done good, unto the resurrection of life; and they that have done evil, unto the resurrection of damnation."

There is to be a resurrection to life and a resurrection to ultimate judgment. The first will be a prelude to eternal bliss, the other to eternal loss. All must rise at His word, and all, without exception, will face one or other of these eternal alternatives.

In rejecting Him, therefore, His accusers were pronouncing condemnation upon themselves and signing their own eternal death warrant.

Never before had Jesus spoken so plainly, and not a word could the rulers find to reply. Furious at the humiliation they had suffered at His hands, they cast about in their minds for some way whereby they might denounce His testimony as false. This was now the only line of attack left to them.

Reading their thoughts, Jesus told them plainly that they would gain nothing by attempting to discount His testimony. If it were unsupported they might conceivably refuse to accept it, but there was a host of witnesses to corroborate His claims.

There was John the Baptist. "Ye sent unto John, and he bare witness unto the truth." He was indeed a "burning and a shining light: and ye were willing for a season to rejoice in his light," that is, until he declared that Jesus was "the Lamb of God, that taketh away the sin of the world." He condemned them because they turned from his witness.

"But," Jesus continued, "I have greater witness than that of John: for the works which the Father hath given Me to finish, the same works that I do, bear witness of Me, that the Father hath sent Me." These works were "signs" to manifest forth His "glory" and to evoke belief in Him. Because the Jews refused to heed them they were condemned by them.

Finally, said Jesus, "Ye search the Scriptures, for in them ye think ye have eternal life." But "they are they which testify of Me, and you will not come to Me, that ye might have life."

"Do not think that I will accuse you to the Father," said Jesus: "there is one that accuseth you, even Moses, in whom ye trust. For had ye believed Moses, ye would have believed Me: for he wrote of Me." Almost the last words which God bade Moses declare to Israel were, "I will raise them up a Prophet from among their brethren, like unto thee, and will put My words in His mouth; and He shall speak unto them all that I shall command Him." The Jews' lack of discernment of the Word had led them to accept a host of false messiahs who had come "in their own name." And now that the true Messiah had come they rejected His incontrovertible witness.

Devastating indeed was Jesus' condemnation of the blindness of the religious leaders. They had rejected God's prophets, God's works, and God's Son. They revealed that they had become the instruments of Satan in his war against heaven.

In that fateful interview, Jesus confronted not only a handful of Jewish leaders with this tremendous witness to His Person. He confronted all men, and each, without exception, must answer for himself the question, "What think ye of Christ?"

Like those Jews, we have the witness of Moses. We have the witness of all the prophets, culminating in the last and greatest of the prophets before Christ, John the Baptist. We have the witness of the works of Jesus from manger to cross and from Calvary to Olivet. And we have also the witness of His works through the Spirit from Pentecost to our day.

Can we refuse to believe that Jesus is the Son of God and our Saviour?

This chapter is based on John 5:16-47.

A Light in the Darkness

THE rejection of Jesus by the Jewish rulers after His miracle at Bethesda was a turning point in His earthly ministry. John's witness had already been silenced by Herod, probably at the instigation of the Pharisees, and now Jesus had a price on His own head. If the death penalty had been within the jurisdiction of the priests Jesus would probably have been sentenced there and then. But His enemies knew that, as a subject people, they could only secure His condemnation by accusing Him of some political crime to the Roman governor. And to obtain grounds for such an accusation they set spies to dog His every step.

In such circumstances there was nothing more that Jesus could do in Jerusalem. His Judean ministry had ended, apparently in failure. Sadly He turned His back on the capital in the late spring of A.D. 29, not again to return until the last six months of His earthly life, when He came to bear His final witness against the city and nation, and to die.

With the close of Jesus' labours in Judea, His Galilean ministry really began. True, He had been in Galilee several times since His baptism. He had spent a few weeks there immediately after the temptation and had performed His first miracle at Cana. He had spent several months there followed His visit to Samaria, waiting for the Passover feast, but little is recorded of His activities during this period, save a second miracle at Cana. During this first year and a half, Galilee had been primarily a place of retirement between the episodes of His Judean labours.

Now that Jesus had been expelled from Jerusalem by the murderous hostility of the religious leaders, Galilee's day of opportunity had come. Says Mark, "Jesus came into Galilee, preaching the Gospel of the kingdom of God, and saying, The

---

Jesus stands at the door of every heart waiting to enter with the light of His blessing and grace.
By HOLMAN HUNT

time is fulfilled, and the kingdom of God is at hand; repent ye, and believe the Gospel."

Matthew describes this new phase of Jesus' ministry thus: "Now when Jesus had heard that John was cast into prison, He departed into Galilee. . . . From that time, Jesus began to preach, and to say, Repent: for the kingdom of heaven is at hand."

Jesus' declaration to the Galileans, "The time is fulfilled," and Matthew's comment, "From that time," are significant. Centuries before, while the children of Israel were languishing in Babylonian captivity, the faithful Daniel, meditating upon God's promise of restoration, was told of the final probationary period of sixty-nine prophetic weeks, or 493 actual years. which would be allotted to the restored nation "to finish

The Bible is light and truth to all who take it as their Guide in life.

the transgression," that is, to forsake every wicked way and come back into perfect harmony with the will of God, in readiness to receive the long-promised Messiah.

It was in fulfilment of this prophetic time period, which began in 457 B.C., that John, the forerunner of Jesus, in the autumn of A.D. 27, made his appeal, "Repent ye: for the kingdom of heaven is at hand." Equally appropriate, therefore, was it for Jesus, as He opened His Galilean ministry, to declare, "The time is fulfilled, repent ye, and believe the Gospel."

There was another Old Testament prophet, even earlier than Daniel, who also made special reference to this Galilean ministry of Jesus.

Just about the time that the apostate northern kingdom of Israel was finally broken up and its peoples were carried away into Assyrian captivity, Isaiah, in the southern kingdom, was inspired to set down a gracious promise of a "great light" which would one day illumine that "land of the shadow of death."

"Nevertheless," he declared, "the dimness shall not be such as was in her vexation, when at the first He lightly afflicted the land of Zebulun and the land of Naphtali, and afterward did more grievously afflict her by the way of the sea, beyond Jordan, in Galilee of the nations." For he declared, prophetically, "The people that walked in darkness have seen a great light: they that dwell in the land of the shadow of death, upon them hath the light shined."

Lower Galilee in the days of Jesus corresponded roughly to the territory occupied by the tribes of Zebulun and Naphtali. Nazareth, where Jesus was to bear His witness at the beginning of His Galilean ministry, was in ancient Zebulun, while Capernaum, which later became the centre of His labours by the Sea of Galilee, was in Naphtali.

Jesus' labours in Galilee began in an atmosphere of unbounded enthusiasm. Everywhere He was eagerly received, and crowds packed the synagogues in which He taught.

Without a doubt, spies from Jerusalem tried to turn the rulers of the synagogues against Him, but at first they had little success, for while there was no suggestion of any lack of orthodoxy in Galilee, these north-country folk did not lay such stress upon the minutiæ of rabbinical tradition, and being closer to the Gentile world they were less bigoted against new ideas.

Furthermore, they were intensely interested in the Messianic hope. Galilee was, in fact, the centre of the Zealot movement founded by Judas of Gamala for the purpose of forcibly overthrowing the Roman tyrants and restoring Jewish independence.

As to whether Jesus was the Messiah or not, there was considerable division of opinion, but they were flattered that a Galilean should have achieved such a reputation. So Jesus was listened to with open minds by eager congregations and, as Luke tells us, "there went out a fame of Him through all the region round about," and He was "glorified of all."

When, however, in the course of His first evangelistic itinerary in Galilee, He came to His home town of Nazareth, it was revealed how transient was the enthusiasm of the excitable Galileans and how quickly it, too, could turn to hatred and rejection.

This chapter is based on Matthew 4:12-17; Mark 1:14, 15; Luke 4:14, 15.

CHAPTER TWENTY-SIX

In the Synagogue of Nazareth

ARRIVING in Nazareth after some weeks of itinerating in Galilee, Jesus went straight to the old home where His mother still lived. How happy Mary was to see her Son again, if only for a brief visit. His brothers and sisters, however, now established in their own homes, had somewhat mixed feelings about Him. They were glad to bask in the reflected glory of His fame, but they were apprehensive about His unorthodoxy and hoped that He was not going to become an embarrassment to the family.

There was a stir of excitement among the inhabitants of the little town on Sabbath morning when they saw Jesus walking with His mother toward the local synagogue.

The remark of the Gospel writer that Jesus went "as His custom was," means more than that it had been His habit since childhood to attend the synagogue on the Sabbath day. It indicates also that, in this phase of His ministry, He regularly availed Himself of the synagogue services to reach the people and deliver His message.

Unlike our churches today, where a regular minister has charge, the synagogues were served by visiting rabbis, or even competent laymen, and any reputable person who had a burden to give a message was given opportunity to speak.

Jesus was therefore able to go from synagogue to synagogue preaching and teaching on Sabbath, and also on the "days of congregation," Monday and Thursday, when the synagogues were open to receive the crowds who came in from the neighbourhood to market.

This gave Him large audiences in every city and village until the religious leaders who had driven Him from the temple were able to induce the elders of the synagogues of Galilee that He was an undesirable person.

The congregation in the synagogue of Nazareth listened entranced to the gracious words of Jesus.
By J. J. TISSOT

The traditional site of the synagogue of Nazareth is on the hillside to the west of the town. Whether it was actually located there we do not, of course, know for certain, but it was customary for the synagogue to be placed, if possible, in an elevated position dominating the community it served. A pilgrim of the sixth century mentions the synagogue as still standing, and in the eleventh century it had been replaced by a church. The present building is not at all ancient, but is still called by the Arabs Medresh el Mesieh, the School of the Messiah.

From the excavation of Jewish synagogues in various parts of Palestine we may conclude that the one at Nazareth comprised a rectangular hall, oriented so that the congregation faced toward Jerusalem, and divided into aisles by rows of pillars extending along its length. Access to the hall would be through a large central door and two smaller ones from a pillared portico or lobby. In a nearby museum are preserved the pedestals of several columns which may very well have come from the synagogue of Jesus' day.

In such a small town as Nazareth, the building would be quite plain with perhaps only a seven-branched candlestick and vine leaves carved over the entrance doorway, but wealthier synagogues, as at Capernaum, had elaborately sculptured symbolic frescoes based upon features of the temple in Jerusalem.

There may have been a gallery above the entrance lobby in which the women sat behind a lattice screen during the services; or the main body of the synagogue may have been divided by lattice work, the women sitting on one side and the men on the other. In many synagogues also there was a separate cubicle where lepers could participate in the services without coming into contact with the rest of the congregation.

At the end of the hall nearest to Jerusalem was a cupboard or ark of painted wood, reached by a flight of steps and covered from sight by a silken draw curtain embroidered with the star of David. Here were stored the sacred scrolls of Scripture, and to simulate the temple a seven-branched candlestick usually stood before it.

Some distance down the centre aisle was an elevated rostrum with a desk from which the Scriptures were read. Upon the rostrum also was a chair called "the chair of Moses," where the preacher for the day sat to give his message.

Around the rostrum were the "chief seats" occupied by the ruler of the synagogue and a quorum of ten elected persons called "men of leisure," whose presence was necessary for the holding of a service. The rest of the congregation occupied the body of the hall, with the children at the back.

The ruler of the synagogue superintended the services, chose the lay readers of the Scriptures, and appointed the preacher or "messenger of the congregation" for the day.

The person who is named the "minister" in the story of Jesus' visit to Nazareth was really the deacon or clerk of the synagogue and was the only paid official. He often also taught in the synagogue school and it was his responsibility to announce the beginning of the Sabbath by three blasts on a silver trumpet from the roof of the synagogue. During the services it was his task to take the sacred scrolls from the ark and to replace them after use.

Such was doubtless the scene in the synagogue at Nazareth as Jesus took His seat in the congregation.

The service opened with several formal prayers read by one of the elders. Then followed the recitation of the Shema, the Jewish equivalent of the creed, based upon several passages from Deuteronomy and Numbers, and further liturgical prayers or eulogies to which the congregation listened standing with bowed heads and hands extended, palms upward, before them. After a benediction all said reverently, "Amen," and sat down.

This brought the first part of the service to an end and led into the second part, which consisted of two Scripture readings. The first was from the law of Moses, a portion being appointed for each service so that the whole of the five books of Moses were read over a period of about three years. On Sabbath seven readers participated in this recital, each taking several verses. The first two readers were always a priest and a Levite, while the others were members of the congregation of known ability to read. For the benefit of those who could not understand Hebrew the readings were interspersed with extempore translations by a Targumist into the local language. In Palestine this would be Aramaic. Elsewhere it might be Greek or some other foreign tongue.

The lesson from the prophets followed, read by only one person and translated as before by the Targumist. Then came the sermon which was given seated by the "messenger" of the day.

It may be that the ruler of the synagogue, having heard that Jesus was in Nazareth had already invited Him to be the "messenger" for that Sabbath, but according to the usual custom, he went over to where Jesus was sitting and formally invited Him to speak. A visiting rabbi would usually go through a little play acting, first declining with mock modesty and then consenting on being pressed. We cannot, however, imagine that Jesus would go through this foolish routine, and when asked He at once rose and followed the ruler to the speaker's rostrum.

From the clerk Jesus received the scroll of the prophet Isaiah, which He had specially requested. Laying it reverently upon the desk He unrolled it to the place where it was written, "The Spirit of the Lord is upon Me, because He hath anointed Me to preach the Gospel to the poor; He hath sent Me to heal the broken-hearted, to preach deliverance to the captives, and recovering of sight to the blind, to set at liberty them that are bruised, to preach the acceptable year of the Lord."

There was a moment of surprise when Jesus finished His reading in the middle of a verse, omitting the remaining phrase, "and the day of vengeance of our God," but they little realized how significant His emphasis on "the acceptable year of the Lord" was to be.

Handing the scroll back to the clerk, Jesus took His seat in the speaker's chair

---

Plates On Next Two Pages: Page 124. The city of Nazareth nestling among the Galilean hills. Page 125. A modern carpenter of Nazareth fashions a wooden plough.

and as He prepared to begin His address, "the eyes of all them that were in the synagogue were fastened on Him."

The congregation at Nazareth had listened to many visiting speakers. They had heard pleasant-voiced popular preachers who flattered their hearers with comfortable platitudes. There had been preachers who held the attention of their congregations by the novelty and ingenuity of their expositions. They had sat through abstruse sermons by erudite visitors, but never had they heard such a commanding speaker, nor a message of such surpassing grace and power as Jesus gave.

Expounding the passage He had read, Jesus described the wondrous work which Messiah was to do, but so different from the usual conception of the Messiah. These Galileans, like most Jews at that time, thought of Messiah as a powerful Leader who would rally the people to His standard, drive out the Roman tyrants, and restore to them their independence. But Jesus showed from the Scriptures that while Messiah would one day overthrow all the enemies of God, His first work was to deliver men from the spiritual tyranny of Satan. He would be concerned to release men not from Roman prisons, but from the prison house of sin. He would open the eyes of the physically afflicted, but He would cure moral and spiritual blindness as well. He would bring the comfort of forgiveness to contrite sinners, and healing to spirits bruised by sorrow and care.

The congregation listened entranced, wondering "at the gracious words which proceeded out of His mouth." Then to their surprise and amazement He declared, "This day is this Scripture fulfilled in your ears."

At once a whispering began to spread among the congregation. What did Jesus mean? Did He claim to be fulfilling, in His own ministry, this Messianic prophecy? Was He asserting that He was the "anointed" Messiah?

"Is not this Joseph's son?" the word began to go round. Why, He was brought up as a boy in their own village. They had known Him from childhood. They had heard strange stories of wonderful works He had done elsewhere, but He would have to give signal evidence of His power before they were prepared to believe that Joseph's son was the Messiah of God!

Jesus sensed the changed feeling that was sweeping the congregation and sadly He said to them, "Ye will surely say unto Me, . . . Whatsoever we have heard done in Capernaum, do also in Thy country. Verily I say unto you, No prophet is accepted in His own country."

For that very reason, Jesus went on to point out, Israel had often missed the blessings which God had for them. In the days of Elijah, because of Israel's unbelief, God had to send His prophet right outside Israel to "Sarepta, a city of Sidon, unto a woman which was a widow" to find shelter until the days of famine were over. Again, in the days of Elisha, the most outstanding miracle that he wrought was not for an Israelite, but for "Naaman the Syrian."

The congregation saw at once what Jesus implied. If they failed to recognize the day of their visitation, they too would be passed by. Their pride was wounded at this plain condemnation of their unbelief, and a storm of protest burst upon Him from all parts of the synagogue. With one accord the congregation arose, thrust Him forth, and with murder in their hearts, drove Him to a hillside overlooking the town.

Visitors to Nazareth often have pointed out to them the so-called Jebel el Qafsah or "Mount of the Leap," a mile to the south of Nazareth, which descends precipitously from a height of nearly 1,300 feet into a deep and narrow gorge. On the summit are the remains of a church with a mosaic pavement and rock-cut altars built there centuries ago to commemorate the tragic occasion. It seems, however, rather unlikely that Jesus would have been taken so far. If the synagogue were near the traditional site it is much more likely that He was driven onto some limestone bluff in the hills to the west.

Wherever the spot was, it seemed as if bodily harm, or even death, must come to Jesus at the hands of the outraged townsfolk. But, as they reached the edge of the declivity, Jesus turned round and faced them. At His gaze they fell back, and as He walked toward them the crowd parted. Not a hand was raised to seize Him. A power greater than themselves seemed to hold them transfixed as calmly He passed through their midst and went His way.

Through the town He walked quickly and out onto the Tiberias road. We can picture Him as He reached the hilltop, looking back for a moment at the city where He had spent so many happy years of childhood and youth, and from which He was now driven away. Was this an omen that Galilee would reject Him as Jerusalem and Judea had done? Sadly He turned His face northward and disappeared over the crest of the hill to seek the shelter of a new home in Capernaum.

How did the family of Jesus relate themselves to the tragic events of this memorable Sabbath? What did they do when the angry congregation rose up against Him? Mary knew that Jesus' claim was true, for the angel Gabriel had told her as much before His birth. But she was powerless to do anything to restrain them, for women were, in no circumstances, allowed to speak in the synagogue.

We know that His brothers did not accept Him as the Messiah, but they must have been alarmed for His safety as the dangerous situation developed, and were greatly relieved when tragedy was averted. Doubtless it was with this near-catastrophe in mind that they persuaded Mary soon after to accompany them to Capernaum to try to restrain Jesus from a course which they were sure would lead Him to disaster and perhaps involve His family as well.

Certainly, they never forgot that Sabbath when Jesus came back to Nazareth, and we can well believe that the memory of the calm with which He faced His persecutors played no small part in their eventual recognition of Him as Saviour and Lord.

This chapter is based on Matthew 4:16-30.

Jesus Finds a New Home

IF Jesus had entertained the thought that Nazareth might serve as a centre for His Galilean ministry, His expulsion from the synagogue revealed conclusively that this was not to be. He could not even go back to visit His mother and brothers without danger of molestation. Now indeed Jesus was homeless. Literally, He had "not where to lay His head."

At once He thought of His fisherman friends in Bethsaida and Capernaum on the shores of the Sea of Galilee, and He turned His steps in that direction. Peter would certainly give Him a welcome and there He could seek guidance from His Father as to His future plans.

On reaching the crest of the mountain range, Jesus paused to look down into the great basin of Galilee. Perhaps it was at that moment, as His eyes ranged over the beautiful and populous region and followed the white lines of the highways which came down to the lakeside, that He was led to the decision that Gennesaret should be the centre of His Galilean ministry.

Excluded from His own town, what could He do better than make some city on the shore of the Sea of Galilee His home? And what more suitable place could He select for this purpose than Capernaum, where all the great highways of Palestine met? From there He would be able to itinerate all over Galilee, and the other side of the lake would be readily accessible by boat. It would be equally easy for those who sought to hear His words or receive His healing touch to come down to the lake. So, as John was led of God to choose one of the busy fords of Jordan for his Judean ministry, Jesus decided that beside the Sea of Galilee He would carry on His work.

Down the Valley of Doves Jesus made His way to Magdala, and then along the

Following the rejection of Jesus in Nazareth, the shores of the Sea of Galilee became the centre of His ministry.

By J. J. TISSOT

coast road to Capernaum and straight to the house of Peter. We can imagine Jesus sadly telling of the happenings in Nazareth, and generous Peter responding by offering Him the hospitality of his home for just as long as He desired.

Gratefully Jesus accepted Peter's kindness and for much of the next year and a half Capernaum was His home. From this time on, more of His recorded discourses were given in the neighbourhood of Capernaum than anywhere else, and many were the miracles He wrought for those who came to Him during His lakeside ministry.

Time and again He returned to Capernaum after His itineraries in Galilee and the Decapolis on the other side of the lake, and when He left it for the last time, it was to go to Jerusalem to suffer and to die.

No wonder Matthew described Capernaum as "His city" and Mark speaks of His being "at home" there.

Capernaum must have been a beautiful place in Jesus' day. Surrounding the city, green pastures and wheatfields, palm and olive groves, fig and pomegranate orchards extended back to the wooded hills, which, in turn, rose to the high plateau of Galilee. How often the pastoral scenes of sowing and reaping, of feeding and watering the flocks, so familiar to the people of the district, provided a backcloth for His wonderful parables. Indeed, it was not far from Capernaum that Jesus described Himself as the "Bread of life."

The blue waters of the lake were dotted with fishing boats, Roman pleasure barges, and war galleys, while dominating the northern horizon across the lake was the mighty, snow-capped peak of Hermon.

On the streets and in the market place of Capernaum was the most cosmopolitan assemblage of humanity to be found anywhere in Palestine, not excepting Jerusalem itself, as travellers and traders of many nationalities mingled with the local population.

From earliest times the Great North Road had come across the volcanic plain of Gaulonitis from Damascus and beyond to the lakeside in Galilee and then on over the hills to the Palestine coast where, under the name of the "Way of the Sea," it ran down into Egypt. Along it the traffic of peace and war had passed since patriarchal days, and in the time of Jesus, Capernaum was a customs post where toll for the maintenance of the great highway was exacted on goods passing north and south.

Southward along the lake shore a road ran down to the Jordan Valley and Gilead, there connecting with the "King's Highway" which traversed ancient Moab, called Perea in the days of Jesus, to the Nabatean kingdom and Arabia.

Across the mountains of Galilee a whole series of roads radiated northwest to Tyre, Sidon, and the ports of Phœnicia, west to Accho, and southwest to Cana, Nazareth, and Esdraelon.

Many were the lessons which Jesus drew, in the course of His teaching, from the merchants and travellers who used these roads, as well as the young adventurers passing through to far countries in search of wealth and pleasure.

Since Capernaum was a garrison town, foot soldiers of the legions, chariots, and horsemen were a familiar sight, and detachments of Roman troops often broke their journey there as they moved to and from the desert frontiers of the Empire. All the world seemed to meet in Capernaum and from it the message of Jesus went north, south, east, and west throughout the land.

Today, at Tell Hum, the ruins of this important fishing port, customs station, and garrison city on the Great North Road extend for almost a mile along the shore of the lake yet, strangely enough, the only distinguishable building is the white marble synagogue which was to figure so largely in the ministry of Jesus.

No-one knows where, among the scattered ruins, stood Peter's house, the home of the generous centurion who built the synagogue, or the customs post where Jesus found Matthew-Levi. But that does not really matter, for as one stands there looking across the plain to the hills and then at the gleaming waters as the sun rises over the brown hills of Gilead, ancient Capernaum becomes as real as if it still stood upon the shores of the beautiful lake.

This chapter is based on Matthew 4:13-17; Luke 4:31.

Jesus leaves His childhood home never to return.
By FURST

CHAPTER
TWENTY-EIGHT

Fishers of Men

A S soon as it became known that Jesus was in Capernaum, crowds began to come
great distances to hear Him. If the news of His rejection in Nazareth had got
around, it certainly had in no way diminished His fame. Soon the local
synagogue was quite inadequate to hold all who came to listen, and Jesus had to
go down to the seaside where large numbers could assemble.

The place to which He resorted may well have been in the vicinity of Tabigha,
for the little bays there form natural amphitheatres ideally suited to the gathering of
the multitudes.

On one particular morning, as the sun came up over the mountains of Gilead
and touched with gold the gleaming waters of the lake, Jesus went down as usual
to the shore. He had little time for quiet communion with His Father before a crowd
gathered. Soon there was so great a throng that He was almost pushed into the
water as He taught.

Looking round, Jesus noticed two fishing boats pulled up on the beach near-by.
One belonged to the brothers Andrew and Simon Peter, and the other to James and
John, who were busily occupied a little distance away.

One might wonder why these disciples were not with the rest of the people
listening to Jesus. But it must be remembered that while on occasions they had
accompanied Jesus on His journeys, they were still earning a living for themselves
and their families as fishermen. They had indeed been out all the preceding night
and now Simon and Andrew, with their long coloured gowns or taliths drawn up
above their knees, were tossing their nets into the sea to rinse off the mud and
weeds, while James and John were mending some of the strands in their nets which

---

Jesus reveals to His fishermen disciples that they are to become "fishers of men."
By ZIMMERMANN   133

had been torn. Even so, they were probably within hearing distance of Jesus, drinking in His words as they worked.

Calling to Peter, whose boat was nearest, Jesus asked him if he would push his craft out a little from the shore. Then, climbing in, Jesus settled Himself in the bows and, as the boat rose and fell on the gentle swell, He continued His discourse.

When Jesus had finished teaching, the crowds dispersed and He was left alone with His fisherman friends. Ever since His expulsion from Jerusalem and the attack made on Him in Nazareth, Jesus recognized that the time was coming when the hatred of the religious leaders would encompass His death. He realized, therefore, that He must begin to train some of His followers so that they could carry on the preaching of the Good News when He was gone. In these four devoted friends, three of whom had been John's staunchest disciples, Jesus saw men eminently qualified to be charter members of that noble company of witnesses. And this was the moment to call them into His service.

Before doing so, however, He wanted to assure them that if they sacrificed home and living for Him, He would not fail in meeting their every temporal need. So, turning to Peter who had just put the clean nets back into his boat, Jesus bade him push out into the deep water and cast them again.

Peter looked incredulously at Jesus. He knew He was not a fisherman by trade and therefore could not be expected to know much about the techniques, but it was fairly common knowledge that the boats always went out at night when the fish came to the surface to feed and could be the more easily caught in the nets. Furthermore, had they not been out all the previous night with most disappointing results, indicating that the shoals had moved to another part of the lake? If they had not found them during the night they were certainly unlikely to be more successful in the daytime.

But Peter had learned to know and love Jesus and he felt in his heart that he must do whatever Jesus asked, however impractical it might seem to him. So, calling his brother Andrew into the boat, he replied, "Master, we have toiled all the night, and have taken nothing: nevertheless at Thy word I will let down the net."

That was what Jesus most wanted to hear. Now He knew that He could rely upon Simon doing whatever He asked him. On His part, He would show Simon that his trust was not misplaced.

No sooner had the big drag nets been cast over the sides of the ship than a great shoal of fish swam right into them and were enclosed as the heavy lead weights dragged the edges of the nets around them. Immediately the boat began to heel over and the nets snapped with the weight of the haul.

Excitedly, Peter and his brother called to James and John who had followed in the other boat, but even with their help the load of fish was almost more than they could take on board, and both boats settled dangerously low in the water.

As they began to move slowly toward the shore Peter remembered his doubts and the grudging way in which he had responded to Jesus' suggestion, and he was overcome with remorse.

Falling at the feet of Jesus he implored Him, "Depart from me; for I am a sinful man, O Lord." He felt that he did not deserve this wonderful thing that Jesus had done for him. Gently Jesus lifted the rough fisherman to his feet. "Fear not," He replied, "from henceforth thou shalt catch men." Peter and his companions had demonstrated their willingness to trust Him completely. Now they were to go with Him and help Him to "catch men alive" in the Gospel "net" for the kingdom of God.

With difficulty the brothers managed to get the two boats to the shore and land the huge catch. But their interest was no longer in the fish. With all their hearts they responded unhesitatingly to the call of the Master. If they could be of service to Him they would leave everything and follow wherever He led.

Readily Zebedee took over the boats and tackle and promised to look after their families when they had to be away with Jesus. And from that time Simon and Andrew, James and John, became the constant companions of Jesus in all His journeys and ministry.

To many it might seem that these first disciples of Jesus were a strange choice. By human standards one would have expected Jesus to choose men of wide education, commanding presence, and powers of oratory for so great a task as founding a church which was to extend to the ends of the earth and endure to the end of time.

But Jesus did not choose by human standards. He looked first for utter devotion to Himself. What these men lacked in worldly wisdom could be more than made up under His divine tutelage. Indeed, not having been schooled in pharisaic tradition, they would have less to unlearn and be the more teachable and ready to receive the truth of God.

Jesus knew, too, that while they could boast none of the culture and dignity of the noble and great, they had, in their hard and perilous calling, learned lessons of diligence and discipline, courage, patience, and endurance, which would stand them in good stead in the arduous service to which He was calling them.

These were the qualities for which Jesus looked in His first disciples, and just such workers He has sought in every generation since to carry the Gospel tidings to their fellow men. True, many from among the wise and noble, like Paul and Nicodemus, Melanchthon and Count Zinzendorf, have dedicated their lives to His service, but the greater number of the heroes of faith have been called from humble and often the lowliest walks of life.

It is not so much fitness for which Jesus looks, as responsiveness to His call, for He is well able to equip and empower those who are ready to serve.

So, whoever you may be, do not feel that you have no talent that He can use. Be assured that as certainly as Jesus is reserving a place in heaven for you, just as certainly has He a place for you in His service on earth. Listen for His call and, like those first disciples by the Galilean sea, be willing to "forsake all" and follow where He leads.

This chapter is based on Luke 5:1-11; Matthew 4:18-22; Mark 1:16-20.

A Busy Sabbath

O N the rising ground of Tell Hum, a little back from the shore of the Sea of Galilee, lie the scattered ruins of ancient Capernaum. Among them can still be clearly traced the outlines of the synagogue in which Jesus taught.

Opinions differ as to whether the present remains are the actual synagogue which stood in the days of Jesus, or a later building, but there is little question that the site is the same and that the general form and construction are identical.

The building was rectangular in shape, like all the synagogues which have been excavated in Palestine, and built of fine white marble blocks. Its size, some seventy by fifty feet, indicates that it was an important synagogue, probably the largest among the lakeside towns. Two rows of columns down the length of the hall, joined by a transverse row at the north end, divided it into a central nave and two narrow side aisles while above was a pillared women's gallery which ran along three sides of the building.

The ark or chest containing the sacred scrolls of Scriptures stood in front of the row of transverse columns until the rabbinical decree that congregations should face toward Jerusalem was enforced, when it was moved to the south end.

Entrance to the building was gained by a large central door and two smaller side doors, each with elaborately carved lintels and friezes.

To one side of the synagogue was a large court with a covered gallery along three sides and a central fountain. This was the synagogue school where the "minister" taught the older boys of Capernaum on week days.

Today only four columns still stand, supporting a length of broken architrave, and grass grows up between the broken stones of the paved court, but the abundant remains of carved Corinthian capitals and ornamental friezes decorated with symbolic

---

Until long into the night Jesus healed and blessed the multitudes who came to Him.
By J. J. TISSOT

motifs like bunches of grapes, pomegranates, and the star and shield of David, witness to the richness of both the interior and exterior of this synagogue built perhaps by the munificence of a Roman officer convert connected with the Capernaum garrison of whom we hear later.

On the first Sabbath after His arrival in the city, Jesus went, "as His custom was," to the synagogue service. Capernaum was agog with excitement and the building was crowded to the doors as Jesus took His seat in one of the places reserved for distinguished guests.

As expected, He was invited by the ruler of the synagogue to give the exhortation, and once again the people were "astonished at His doctrine: for He taught them as one that had authority, and not as the scribes." Unlike His fellow townsmen in Nazareth, however, the congregation in Capernaum received His word with gladness and rejoicing of heart. For not only had His fame reached them from the upland towns He had visited, but the nobleman of Capernaum whose little boy Jesus had healed some time before, had made no secret of His devotion to the Master.

We have no record of the passage which Jesus read that Sabbath morning, nor of the content of His sermon, but we may be sure that, as always, His theme was of God's love for sinners, the salvation made available to them by His grace, and the promise of the kingdom.

To a congregation wearied by the long and tedious discourses of the scribes, the great truths which Jesus expounded came with an authority which stimulated their minds and stirred their hearts as never before.

Never had they listened to a teacher with such an insight into human nature or so profound an understanding of the purposes of God.

Never had they recognized the sinfulness of sin or the transforming power of grace in heart and life as it was portrayed to them by Him who had come down from heaven "full of grace and truth."

The message of Jesus was so clear, so convincing, so urgent, that His hearers could not but respond to its appeal and power.

Jesus was drawing to the close of His discourse when suddenly a piercing shriek drowned His words. A gaunt, unkempt figure with dishevelled hair and staring eyes flung himself forward and fell at the foot of the raised platform on which Jesus stood. From his foaming lips burst the defiant cry: "Let us alone; what have we to do with Thee, Thou Jesus of Nazareth? art Thou come to destroy us? I know Thee who Thou art, the Holy One of God."

In our so-called scientific age it is common to explain away this and other references to spirit possession in the Bible as the result of ignorance of medical psychology. But if we do this we ascribe ignorance to Jesus, too, for on many occasions He referred to the existence of fallen spirits, and He clearly recognized the possibility of their "possessing" those who yielded themselves to their power.

The Bible means what it says when it declares that this tragic creature was "demonized." Today Satan may use subtler means to control his human dupes, but those who have taken the Gospel among primitive peoples know that demon-possession is still a terrible reality.

The poor man had somehow crept into the synagogue unobserved, and as he listened to Jesus a great yearning came into his heart to be free from the spirit which held him captive in its evil grip. He tried to make known his longing to Jesus, but the spirit strove to hold his victim in his power.

Despite his simulated defiance, however, the evil intelligence knew that Jesus was the incarnate Son of God who had come to earth "to destroy the works of the devil" and to set his "prisoners" free.

The fears of the unclean spirit were well founded, for Jesus, looking with pity into the pleading eyes of the tortured soul, peremptorily ordered the spirit to hold his peace and leave the man.

Convulsing his victim in a final paroxysm, the spirit obeyed and fled to his evil master. In an instant the man's writhings ceased and he stood to his feet restored and calm.

The congregation were awestruck at the miracle. They had seen or heard of many evidences of the power of Jesus. He had demonstrated His power over nature by turning water into wine. He had rebuked disease and made the sick well. But here was a power they had never expected to see, for, they said, "With authority commandeth He even the unclean spirits, and they do obey Him."

What Jesus had done was only a fulfilment of the word spoken prophetically of Him by Isaiah: "Even the captives of the mighty shall be taken away, and the prey of the terrible shall be delivered: for I will contend with him that contendeth with thee, and I will save thy children."

It was yet another sign to men that Jesus was the omnipotent Son of God, and it was a warning to Satan that he had no power but what he was permitted to exercise. It assures us, too, that though, in these last days, the devil may go forth "having great wrath, because he knoweth that he hath but a short time," and reduce millions to abject submission, the day is surely coming when his career will be cut short and he himself will perish!

As the amazed congregation scattered, the news of this latest miracle was quickly carried far and wide among "all the region round about Galilee."

Leaving the synagogue Jesus went back to the house of Simon, and of course Andrew, James, and John went with Him, for now they were inseparable from their Master.

Simon's wife's mother had not been at the service that morning for she was very ill with a sudden prostrating attack, probably of malaria, which is common in the sub-tropical climate of the Galilee basin. Luke's use of a technical term translated "great fever" incidentally reveals his knowledge of medicine, for he was a physician. Neither Peter nor his wife had mentioned their mother's condition to Jesus because they knew that He was to teach in the synagogue, but when He was refreshed from the strain of the morning they told Him of their anxiety.

At once Jesus rose and went to her. It may be she had been brought into Peter's

ABOVE

The Jordan River winding through a tropical jungle between fantastically eroded limestone cliffs.

LEFT

The Jordan valley near the traditional site of John the Baptist's ministry and the baptism of Jesus.

OPPOSITE

The "Mount of Temptation" in the Wilderness of Judea near Jericho and the Jordan ford.

house so that his wife could better look after her. Stooping low, Jesus took her tenderly by the hand and raised her up. As He did so the fevered flush was dissipated, her brow became cool, and her strength returned.

Immediately she arose from her couch and began helping her daughter to minister to the needs of their guests. Her gratitude was shown in deeds, not just in words.

Jesus spent the rest of the Sabbath afternoon quietly in Peter's house, but everywhere in Capernaum and the neighbouring villages the excitement was intense. Hope sprang up in the hearts of all the sick and afflicted that the Great Physician might heal them also. Had it not been for the rabbinical prohibitions on travel and the seeking of physical relief during the Sabbath hours, they would have crowded into the city at once. But fear of reproof from the Pharisees restrained them.

As soon as the sun had gone down, however, a great trek along the roads into Capernaum began. Some shuffled painfully along leaning heavily upon staves or crutches. Others rode upon asses or were borne on rough litters. Parents mingled with the crowd carrying their sick infants. Here and there poor demented creatures, like the demoniac in the synagogue, were led along by friends who hoped that Jesus might cast out the evil spirits which possessed them. Soon the courtyard of Simon's house was crowded with sufferers and many more thronged the street outside.

The heart of Jesus was filled with sympathy as He went out among the motley multitude. Gently He laid His hands upon the sick and, at His touch, faces lighted up with relief from racking pain, cripples threw away their crutches, blind eyes opened, the dumb spoke, and the shrieks of the possessed were turned to pæans of gratitude and praise.

Far into the night Jesus worked and the moon stood high over the silver waters of the lake as the last of the sufferers were sent back to their homes well and happy. But long after the streets had emptied and the doors of the houses were shut, rejoicing could be heard in countless homes. For there was not one sick person left in all Capernaum and its neighbourhood. Jesus had healed them "every one."

That wonderful night is not just a memory of the distant past. The Great Physician may no longer walk visibly among men, but His touch has still its ancient power. His sympathy goes out to sufferers in every land today. He longs for the afflicted in body, mind, and spirit to come to Him, and His promise still holds good, "Who forgiveth all thine iniquities; who healeth all thy diseases."

There were, of course, times when Jesus saw that it was best for suppliants who came to Him to endure the ills of the flesh that they might learn lessons of dependence and trust. The apostle Paul tells how three times he pleaded in vain that his "thorn in the flesh" might be removed. And in God's wisdom, it may be so with us. But whenever it is not in His purpose

to heal, He gives, as He did to Paul, grace sufficient to bear the burden, and bids us patiently await the day when the Great Physician will "wipe away" all the tears that remain, and "there shall be no more death, neither sorrow, nor crying, neither shall there be any more pain."

This chapter is based on Mark 1:21-34; Luke 4:31-41; Matthew 8:14-17.

At home and abroad devoted doctors and nurses are carrying on the work of the Great Physician.

By M. FEUERSTEIN

A Leper Cleansed

THOUGH Jesus had worked long into the night after His busy Sabbath in Capernaum, He was up before dawn and walking quickly through the silent streets to a quiet spot outside the city to commune with His Father in prayer.

Jesus had no sin to confess, nor any forgiveness to seek, but when He said, "I can of Mine own self do nothing," He revealed His utter dependence upon God. All He gave forth He received from His Father. In the secret place of prayer He sought guidance for each day and strength to meet its demands and trials. There, too, He interceded for those to whom He would bring the Word of life.

Jesus was never too busy to pray. The more pressed He was, the more assiduously He sought and maintained prayer intercourse with His Father. And in the supreme crises of His life He would often spend whole nights in communion.

What an example to us who so often offer the excuse of our manifold tasks for the neglect of private devotions. If we would live as Jesus lived, and labour as He laboured, we must pray as He prayed. For prayer is the secret of the life of victory.

As soon as it was light the crowds began to gather again, but when they inquired after Jesus, He was nowhere to be found. Peter, however, guessed where He would be and led the more eager of the people to His secret retreat.

Jesus rose from His knees as they approached. Excitedly, Peter ran up to Him. "All men seek for Thee," he cried.

Peter's impetuosity was well intentioned enough. The people were looking for Jesus and he knew that the Master could meet all their needs. He just wanted to bring them together as speedily as possible.

But Jesus had other plans. While the people of Capernaum would have been very happy if Jesus had consented to remain among them, He knew that

---

On the outskirts of the city a poor leper came pleading for Jesus' healing touch.
By J. J. TISSOT

He was sent not just to the people of one city, but "to all men" everywhere. So, resisting their endeavours to "stay" Him, He said to Peter, "Let us go into the next towns, that I may preach there also: for therefore came I forth."

And so began, in the early summer of A.D. 29, the first major missionary itinerary of Jesus which took Him "throughout all Galilee," where He preached "in their synagogues," and healed all who came to Him.

Of all the wonderful happenings that could have been recorded of this Galilean journey, only one incident has been preserved, but it is not difficult to understand why it should have been chosen by the pen of Inspiration.

Jesus came to a "certain" but unnamed city. He had no doubt preached in the synagogue and healed many in the streets, and was about to leave for the next town when He was met on the outskirts by a leper. Leprosy was the most terrible of the diseases that afflicted the world of Jesus' day. No cure was known for the dread contagion which gradually ate away the flesh and bones of its victims, until, reduced to a putrid mass of corruption, they finally succumbed.

All that could be done was to banish the leper, be he commoner or king, from human society to prevent his passing the disease on to others. No clean person would approach within six feet of him. Whatever he touched was contaminated. He was refused entry into any city and was condemned to wander in uninhabited places, his head swathed so that only his eyes showed, and crying "Unclean, unclean," to the day of his lonely and horrible death.

So fearful indeed was the disease and its consequences, that the Jews regarded it as a direct judgment from God. They called it "the finger of God" and had a proverb, "As God sends leprosy so God alone can heal it." This explains the expostulation of the king of Israel when the king of Syria sent Naaman the leper to him: "Am I God, . . . that this man doth send unto me to recover a man of his leprosy?"

What a challenge it was, therefore, to the claims of Jesus, when one of these poor stricken creatures, in an advanced stage of the disease, "full of leprosy," as the physician Luke mentions, fell at His feet in humble supplication.

He was indeed a loathsome sight. His skin was cracked and blistered. His fingers and toes were already partly eaten away, and his face was horribly marred.

How much he had heard of the miracles of Jesus, we do not know but, by some inward prompting of the Spirit, he was confident that the great Healer could cleanse even a leper if He would. The only fear in His heart was whether, under the judgment of God, he had a right to ask anything of One so pure and holy. But in deep humility he cast himself upon the mercy of Jesus, crying, "If Thou wilt, Thou canst make me clean."

The crowd fell back horrified at his close approach, but Jesus showed no repugnance. Alienated from his fellowmen he might be, but not from the ever-compassionate Jesus.

To the amazement of the crowd He stretched forth His hand and touched the poor sufferer, saying as He did so, "I will; be thou clean." "And as soon as He had spoken, immediately the leprosy departed from him, and he was cleansed." His skin became smooth and fresh as a little child's and the look of utter desolation was turned to radiant joy. Little wonder that the onlookers were staggered at the miraculous transformation.

Then Jesus said a strange thing. "See thou say nothing to any man," He bade the healed leper. If His miracles were for "signs," what could be the reason for this unexpected stipulation?

According to the Mosaic ordinances it was necessary for a leper who had been cleansed, to obtain from a priest a certificate of cleanness before he could associate again with his fellow men. If the mind of the local priest had been poisoned against Jesus by His Pharisee enemies, he might easily have refused to pronounce the man clean. This would have brought disappointment to the leper and would have seemed to cast disrepute upon the work of Jesus.

So, to avoid any possibility of arousing prejudice and opposition, Jesus told the man to say nothing to anyone about how he had been cleansed, but to go straight to the priest, secure the legal certificate of cleanness, and then proceed to the temple and offer the prescribed sacrifices in gratitude for his restoration.

If, after that, it became known that he had been cleansed by Jesus, it would be a "testimony" on the one hand to the source of His power and on the other, it would refute the accusation made against Jesus at the Pool of Bethesda that He set aside the law of Moses and encouraged others to do so. For until type met Antitype on the cross, it was not His purpose that any of the symbolic ordinances of the sanctuary should be set aside. From Jordan to Calvary Jesus "fulfilled all righteousness" until all righteousness was fulfilled in Him.

Instead, however, of heeding the warning of Jesus, the healed leper "went out, and began to publish it much, and to blaze abroad the matter." In a way one can understand the desire of one who had been delivered from so fearful an affliction to broadcast the fact, but it would have been far better if he had shown his gratitude by obedience. For, as a result of his indiscretion, Jesus "could no more openly enter into the city," but was compelled to retire to the country for a time.

It may be that Jesus was regarded as defiled by His contact with the leper and forbidden entrance to the city by the authorities, or He may have been excluded for fear that He might draw many lepers to the city and so endanger the safety of the inhabitants. In either case the man's indiscretion made the work of Jesus in that place more difficult. But in the providence of God the mistake was overruled, for "great multitudes came together" in the desert "to hear, and to be healed by Him of their infirmities."

The healing of this poor leper was yet another signal demonstration of the power of Jesus to heal "all manner of sickness, and all manner of disease" among the people. But it was much more. It was vividly illustrative of His even greater work of cleansing away the spiritual leprosy of sin.

Leprosy, more than any other disease, typifies the moral pollution of sin. Both the leper and the sinner are described in the Scriptures by the same term, "unclean."

Sin, like leprosy, is often no more than a minute blemish on the character in its beginnings, but when it has fastened its victim in its grip it penetrates to every thought, word, and action until "from the sole of the foot even unto the head there is no soundness in it; but wounds, and bruises, and putrifying sores." The victim of sin, like the leper, is "dead" while he "liveth."

Leprosy was not a disease of one class of society. It struck the poor man in his hovel and the king on his throne. And so does sin.

The leper was alienated from his fellow men, but sin alienates from God. "Your iniquities," He declares, "have separated between you and your God, and your sins have hid His face from you, that He will not hear." No "unclean" sinner may enter the city of God. Before him is the prospect of everlasting banishment.

Only God could cleanse the leper and only God can deliver the sinner from the curse of sin.

But Jesus loves the sinner, no matter how vile, as He loved the loathsome leper. He is not only able but willing to save all who come, in humble supplication, to Him. And the contagion of sin yields instantly to His healing touch.

The ceremony of cleansing which the priest carried out on behalf of the healed leper likewise beautifully portrays the sinner's release from the bondage of sin. The priest was commanded to take two unblemished birds. One he killed, allowing its blood to flow into a vessel of water, signifying the redeeming sacrifice of Christ.

The other bird was bound together with a sprig of hyssop to a cedar stick by means of a scarlet thread. It was then dipped by the priest into the bowl of mingled blood and water and sprinkled seven times upon the body of the cleansed leper. This symbolically transferred to him the merits of the shed blood.

The live bird was finally released to fly back among its fellows, symbolizing the release of the leper from his banishment.

What a wonderful picture this presents of sinners cleansed by the "blood" of Christ and rising from the "waters" of baptism to new life and fellowship with Him.

Eight days after this ceremony another completed the symbolism. Following the sacrifice of a he-lamb as a trespass offering, some of the blood was put upon the right ear, the right thumb, and the right great toe of the healed leper, the process being then repeated with the oil of the wave offering. All this typified the restoration of privilege to the leper to hear, touch, and walk freely among men. In like manner the application of the blood, through the Spirit, restores the sinner to fellowship with God and with His people.

As we ponder this miracle and the symbolic cleansing ceremony which followed it, we understand more clearly the terrible nature of sin and the wonder of the redemption offered us through Christ.

This chapter is based on Mark 1:35-45; Luke 5:12-16; Matthew 8:2-4.

CHAPTER
THIRTY-ONE

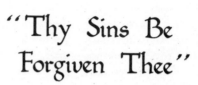

"Thy Sins Be Forgiven Thee"

JESUS was back again in Capernaum after His missionary itinerary through Galilee. Quickly the news went around and the multitudes flocked to Peter's house to hear Him. The room in which He sat was soon filled to the doors and the courtyard was thronged with people straining to catch the Teacher's words through the open window.

But not all who were there were seeking a blessing at His hands. Among those nearest to Jesus were "Pharisees and doctors of the law" who had come with the deliberate purpose of seeking evidence against Him. The fact that some of them "were come out of . . . Judea and Jerusalem" shows that representatives had been sent from the capital to incite the leaders in Galilee against Jesus. They may have had a part in the disturbance in Nazareth, but as yet they had not dared to criticize Him openly in Capernaum, for Jesus was a popular hero there. Jesus recognized His critics, but He went on teaching as if unconscious of their presence.

As the people listened intently to Him, four men came through the outer gate bearing on a mattress a helpless paralytic. They tried to push their way through the crowd to Jesus, but it was impossible. Just as they were about to turn away disappointed one of them had an idea. Why not go up onto the flat roof and see if there was a section left loose for opening during the hot summer days? If so, their friend could be let down through this to Jesus.

Acting at once on the excellent suggestion, the men carefully ascended the stone stairway in one corner of the courtyard and reached the roof over the room where Jesus sat. As they expected, they found in the centre a square of loose laths covered with matting and tiles. Removing these they drew the laths to one side. Soon they had made an opening large enough to pass the mattress and patient through.

149

By this time the people in the room below were gazing up to see what was happening, and when the four resourceful friends lowered the man down through the hole, many pairs of hands were raised to bring him gently to the floor.

As Jesus looked up at the men who had overcome all obstacles to bring their friend to Him, His heart was touched by their faith. But while their hopes were primarily for the physical restoration of the paralytic, Jesus saw in his imploring eyes an even greater need. The plight of the paralytic was the result of the sinful abuse of his body and in his upturned face Jesus discerned a sorrow, not of remorse but of true repentance. His speechless lips moved as if to say, with the Psalmist, "Heal my soul; for I have sinned against Thee."

This was what Jesus most desired to do for those who came to Him. He wanted to deliver men, not merely from the consequences, but from the power, of sin. He was the Great Physician of the soul as well as of the body.

On earlier occasions like this it had been the practice of Jesus first to heal the repentant ones and then bid them, "Go, and sin no more." But this time, because He knew that the Pharisees and lawyers were seeking an occasion against Him, He fearlessly chose to reveal the fullness of His authority and power.

Addressing Himself to the man's deep spiritual need Jesus said, "Son, . . . thy sins be forgiven thee."

The words were spoken with an authority quite different from that of a priest in the temple pronouncing absolution in the name of God. Jesus was speaking, not for God, but as God, and immediately a look of peace and content overspread the sufferer's drawn face.

Raising His eyes from the still prone form of the paralytic,

Removing the loose laths and matting they made an opening large enough to let their patient down to Jesus in the room below.

By Wm. HOLE

Jesus looked across at the Pharisees in the corner of the room. The malicious glint in their eyes told Him that the import of His words had not been lost upon them. Reading their thoughts as easily as He had read the thoughts of the repentant paralytic, He knew they were saying to themselves, "Why doth. this Man thus speak blasphemies? who can forgive sins but God alone?"

This was just the kind of evidence that they sought. John had announced Jesus as the Messiah for whom the nation was looking, but they could not condemn Him simply on John's testimony.

Jesus had claimed God as His Father when He had appeared before the Sanhedrin after the miracle at Bethesda. That was valuable evidence out of His own mouth, but what they really wanted was proof of His actually assuming the prerogatives of God. Now they had it. They had heard Him actually claiming the power to forgive sin, a right which belonged to God alone.

Jesus read all this in their gloating looks and their significant glances at one another. Answering their unspoken accusation, He said, "Why reason ye these things in your hearts? Whether is it easier to say to the sick of the palsy, Thy sins be forgiven thee; or to say, Arise, and take up thy bed, and walk?"

He had as much right to say the one as the other, and as this man's affliction was the result of his sin, it was entirely appropriate that He should deal with this first. As, however, they doubted His authority to forgive the sin, He would now give them tangible evidence of it by removing the affliction resulting from the sin.

And turning again to the paralytic He said, "I say unto thee, Arise, and take up thy bed, and go thy way into thine house." No sooner had He spoken, than the man "rose up before them and took up that whereon he lay," and, as the crowd parted to allow him to pass, he "departed to his own house, glorifying God."

Jesus could have given no more convincing evidence "that the Son of man hath power on earth to forgive sins." If He had been only a man acting for God and had sinfully assumed divine prerogatives as Moses did when he struck the rock in the wilderness, God would have rebuked Him as He rebuked Moses. That God permitted the completion of the miracle clearly showed that Jesus had not spoken falsely but that, as the divine Son, He shared His authority.

No wonder that all who witnessed the miracle were "amazed," and "filled with fear" sensing, though without full comprehension, that the Son of man they saw before them must also be the "Son of God."

"We have seen strange things today," they said one to another as they went out. But the hearts of the Pharisees and lawyers were steeled against the convincing proof Jesus had given of His true nature. Their hatred of Him, and their opposition to Him, were now irrevocable. They were completely in Satan's hands and determined to watch Him unceasingly until they had all the evidence they needed to secure His condemnation and death.

This chapter is based on Mark 2:1-12; Luke 5:17-26; Matthew 9:2-8.

CHAPTER THIRTY-TWO

The Call
of Matthew

O N the shore of the Sea of Galilee between the ruins of Tell Hum, the site of
ancient Capernaum, and the bay of Tabigha, there are to be seen some
massive hewn stones which look very much like a harbour wall. If this is
so, then quite near here stood the "place of toll" or harbour customs house in the
charge of Levi, the Jew.

He was one of a considerable class of officials called publicans, who were
responsible for the collection of taxes for Herod Antipas, tetrarch of Galilee and
Perea. And as Capernaum was the chief port at the northern end of the Sea of
Galilee and a great road junction as well, the revenue collected there must have
been considerable.

On the roads coming into Capernaum from the north there were "places of toll"
where duty was exacted on all traffic from Damascus and the north. This was usually
in the region of two and a half to five per cent on the value of the goods in transit,
with higher taxes on luxuries.

Levi, in the harbour customs office, collected harbour dues and the duty on all
goods brought by ship from the other side of the Sea of Galilee. Much of these
cargoes would be grain, as the fertile basalt plateau of Gaulanitis was one of the
granaries of the Middle East in the time of Jesus.

In the towns and villages of the Gennesaret plain there were other tax offices,
with probably a central department in Capernaum, concerned with the collection of
tribute from the local population. This included poll tax, income tax, and a ground
tax paid in kind, normally a tithe of grain crops and a fifth of the wine produced.

As a class the publicans were regarded with hatred and execration by the Jews.

To Levi's surprise, Jesus came straight up to the toll booth to speak to him.
By J. J. TISSOT

This is reflected by the frequent references in the gospels to "publicans and sinners," both apparently equally deserving of detestation.

That Jews could sink so low as to collect tribute from their own countrymen for their foreign overlords, whether the Roman procurator in Judea or the pro-Roman puppet Herod in Galilee, was enough to condemn them as renegades and traitors. But this was not their only crime. For it was known that over and above the revenue which they were required to pass on to their masters they all fraudulently enriched themselves by unjust extortion and partiality. With good cause they were designated "mokhes" or "oppressors," and it was the resistance of the Jews to this iniquitous taxation which precipitated the final revolt in the days of Vespasian and Titus, and brought about their complete overthrow.

Such was the general feeling against publicans that they were, in no circumstances, allowed to serve as judges in the communities where they lived, and their witness was unacceptable in the law courts. They were also excluded from the synagogues as apostates.

Even the Greek writer Artimidorus, who had none of the religious prejudices of Jesus, a great longing came into his heart to give up his lucrative but questionable warned against taking a wife "from the family of a publican."

To this universally execrated class Levi belonged. But though despised and shunned by his fellow countrymen he did not escape the notice of Jesus. For whenever He passed by on His way to the seashore, Jesus observed that Levi would come out of the toll house and stand on the edge of the crowd to listen.

Levi had been put to the profession of tax officer doubtless by a publican father, but his better feelings had never been entirely submerged. As he drank in the words of Jesus, a great longing came into his heart to give up his lucrative but questionable profession and live a better life. But it was almost more than he could expect that the great Teacher would concern Himself about a despised publican.

To Jesus, however, there were no social barriers, and when He saw the transformation that was going on in Levi's heart, He determined to put his kindling faith to the test.

On this particular morning, Levi saw Jesus approaching and, as he was not too busy, he decided to go out to hear Him once more. Great was his surprise, however, when he saw Jesus stop at the toll booth and come straight in. As their eyes met Levi knew why Jesus had come, and when He uttered the simple but challenging words, "Follow Me," without a moment's hesitation Levi arose and went out with Jesus. What he had not dared to hope had come to pass. Jesus was willing to receive a publican as one of His disciples.

Of course, Levi had to slip back to the customs house when Jesus finished teaching, to clear up his affairs and delegate his responsibilities, but from that day he forsook the work in which he had engaged for so many years and dedicated his life to Jesus and His cause.

The people who came regularly to listen to Jesus must have been very surprised and shocked when they saw that Jesus had called a publican into the company of

His disciples, and the disciples themselves may have had their doubts about him at first. But when they saw the genuine change which had taken place in his life they welcomed him into their fellowship.

Just as Jesus renamed Simon when he became a disciple, He marked this new beginning in Levi's life by giving him a new name, Matthew, meaning "gift of God." This was indeed appropriate, for God had given salvation to Levi and in return Levi had given himself and all his talents to God. With the possible exception of Nathaniel, Matthew was the most educated of the disciples whom Jesus had so far called, and after his Master's death it was the consecrated pen of Matthew which wrote one of the first accounts of His life and teachings.

This chapter is based on Mark 2:13, 14; Luke 5: 27, 28; Matthew 9:9.

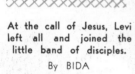

At the call of Jesus, Levi left all and joined the little band of disciples.

By BIDA

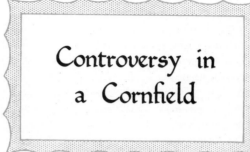

Controversy in a Cornfield

IT was a Sabbath in early June, A.D. 29, and the ripening wheatfields around
the Sea of Galilee were a picture of gold in a frame of wooded green hills.

Jesus had been visiting a synagogue a little distance from Capernaum and was
returning by a path through the waving corn. Neither He nor His companions had
eaten since early morning and they were hungry.

When the disciples saw the tall ripe ears bending before the breeze they availed
themselves of the permission granted in one of the kindly laws of Moses, and plucked
a few to eat as they walked. "When thou comest into the standing corn of thy neighbour," God had said, "then thou mayest pluck the ears with thine hand."

Following Jesus, as usual, were some of the Pharisee spies, and when they
observed the disciples plucking the corn and rubbing away the chaff between their
palms they saw a new opportunity for complaint. For while there was nothing in
the Mosaic law to forbid such an act on the Sabbath day, the supplementary ordinances devised by the Pharisees condemned it as Sabbath-breaking. "He that reapeth
corn on the Sabbath to the quantity of a fig is guilty," declared one regulation, while
another stated very specifically, "plucking is as reaping." Still another ordinance declared
that rubbing grain between the fingers was the equivalent of threshing. So the
disciples were culpable on two counts.

Approaching Jesus in protest, they asked Him, "Behold, why do" Thy disciples
"on the Sabbath day that which is not lawful?"

If Jesus had replied that He did not recognize the multiplicity of rules with
which they had hedged the Sabbath about, the Pharisees would immediately have
accused Him of undermining spiritual discipline, but He did not fall into this
obvious trap.

Often Jesus walked to nearby villages to heal and to teach in the synagogues.

By J. J. TISSOT

Instead, He asked them a question which exposed their complete lack of comprehension of the true intent of the Sabbath law. "Have ye never read," Jesus said, "what David did, when he had need, and was an hungered, he, and they that were with him?"

The occasion to which He referred was when David was fleeing from the wrath of Saul with some of his faithful companions. Because they had been compelled to keep away from inhabited places they had run out of food and were hungry. So, leaving them in a lonely cave, David made his way to the priestly city of Nob, some miles north-east of Jerusalem. Meeting Ahimelech the priest, David asked him for food. Ahimelech replied that he had none except the loaves of showbread which had just been taken from the table in the sanctuary and replaced by twelve fresh loaves.

David explained his great need and begged that the showbread be given him. If Ahimelech had been a Pharisee he would have told David that the showbread was set apart expressly for the priests and in no circumstances could he allow David to have any of it.

But Ahimelech did not oppose any such arguments to David's plea. When he recognized that this was an unanticipated emergency he immediately gave him the hallowed bread.

This incident from the Scriptures put the Pharisees on the horns of a dilemma. They dared not suggest that Ahimelech did wrong in giving the showbread to David, for he was an honoured priest of God, and they could not condemn David for asking for it, for he was the most revered of the kings of Israel. On the other hand, if they admitted that Ahimelech and David did no wrong, they could hardly sustain their criticism of the disciples of Jesus in similar need.

Chagrined and embarrassed, they would have dropped the subject forthwith, but Jesus added to their confusion by another question.

"Have ye not read in the law," He asked, "how that on the Sabbath days the priests in the temple profane the Sabbath, and are blameless?" They knew perfectly well that, for the priests, the Sabbath was the busiest day of the week. They had to kindle fires, an act prohibited to the common people. They had to dress and prepare the sacrifices, though it was unlawful for the Israelites to prepare food in their homes. The Pharisees knew that these acts were not a violation of the Sabbath because they were in the spiritual interests of Israel. In like manner the hunger of the disciples had been incurred by the extended ministry of Jesus, and if He found no fault with them, who were the Pharisees to criticize?

If they had known their Bibles, Jesus told them, they would have remembered the admonition of God through Hosea, "I desired mercy, and not sacrifice," and they would have recognized that there was no virtue in a meticulous adherence to the letter of the law but complete unconcern for the welfare of others.

Sacrifices, burnt offerings, and every procedure associated with the temple worship, were important. They were instituted for a symbolic purpose, and until type met Antitype on the cross, they were obligatory upon Israel. But they were only typical acts and did not take precedence over the positive requirements of practical godliness.

The trouble with the whole pharisaic system was that conformity to the requirements of the law had been exalted into an end in itself, to the exclusion of concern for the necessities of their fellow men.

Jesus was trying to show these legalists that to practise the letter while violating the spirit of the law was to make a mockery of what was intended to inculcate moral virtue and love.

To concentrate on the externals of Sabbath observance and to forget its inner meaning was to miss completely the blessing it offered to men.

This chapter is based on Mark 2:23-28; Matthew 12:1-8; Luke 6:1-5.

As the disciples walked through a field of ripe corn they picked a few ears and ate them.
By E. ARMITAGE

CHAPTER THIRTY-FOUR

Lord of the Sabbath

NOT long after the incident in the cornfield Jesus had another clash with the Pharisees on what was proper Sabbath observance.

He had gone into the synagogue as was "His custom" and was about to take His seat when the Pharisees who were present drew His attention to a poor man whose withered right arm hung limp and helpless at his side.

Bluntly they asked Jesus: "Is it lawful to heal on the Sabbath days?" They knew that already on the Sabbath He had healed the impotent man at the pool of Bethesda, the demoniac in the synagogue at Capernaum, and Peter's wife's mother, and they hoped for a declaration from His own lips which they could use to condemn Him. But, as on other occasions, Jesus replied with another question.

Calling the man to stand forth, He asked the Pharisees: "Is it lawful to do good on the Sabbath days, or to do evil? to save life, or to kill?"

Now it was their turn to be embarrassed. They could hardly say that it was ever unlawful to do good, but if they conceded the point to Jesus they would undermine their own tradition. So they said nothing.

Following up the advantage of their silence, Jesus proceeded to expose the under-lying selfishness of their supposed high principles.

"What man shall there be among you," He said, "that shall have one sheep, and if it fall into a pit on the Sabbath day, will he not lay hold on it, and lift it out?"

According to the Pharisees, such an act was justified on the grounds that if nothing were done, greater harm might come to the animal. In reality, it was a loop-hole to avoid financial loss. The continued suffering of a human being, on the other hand, could not touch them in any way so they were unconcerned about its alleviation.

Grieved and indignant at their callousness, Jesus demanded: "How much then

For healing the man with the withered arm on the Sabbath, Jesus was severely criticized by the bigoted Pharisees.

By J. J. TISSOT

is a man better than a sheep?" and without waiting for their reply He turned to the man with the withered arm, and said to him, "Stretch forth thine hand."

As the poor man had listened to the discussion between Jesus and the Pharisees he recognized the power and authority of the great Teacher's words, and although he had never been able so much as to move his arm for years he was impelled to obey. Immediately, in response to his faith, the long-dead muscles tautened, every sign of wasting vanished, and it became "whole, like as the other."

By this miracle in the synagogue Jesus once again stressed the fundamental principle underlying the Sabbath commandment which He had enunciated in His controversy with the Pharisees in the cornfield: "The Sabbath was made for man, and not man for the Sabbath."

When the seventh day was set apart and hallowed at the end of the creation week it was intended by God for man's benefit and blessing. The work of the week was to be so planned in field and workshop and home that when the Sabbath hours came, all, including the servants and the beasts of burden, might rest and be physically refreshed.

The Sabbath was also to serve an important spiritual purpose, for, being freed from the manifold duties of the working week, man would have leisure to meditate upon the wonderful provisions of God in creation and seek communion with Him through worship. Thus for all time all men everywhere would keep in mind the Source of all their benefits. Also, as occasion afforded, they could use the opportunity of the Sabbath rest to show their thankfulness by deeds of love and service to their fellow men.

How important a purpose the Sabbath was to serve is indicated by the fact that it was included in the "Ten Commandments" which God gave to Israel on Sinai as the epitome of His law.

By His teaching and His example Jesus sought to reveal the true purpose of the law of God and to restore to man the special blessing of the Sabbath rest, which the Pharisees had made into a burden.

That Jesus had every right to make known the purpose of the Sabbath, He made very clear when He reminded His critics, "The Son of man is Lord also of the Sabbath day."

As God's agent in creation it was He who instituted the Sabbath at the close of the creation week, and as His mouthpiece on Sinai it was He who enshrined the Sabbath in the "ten words" of the Decalogue. Obviously then, His word was authoritative as to the manner of its observance, and it was the height of impertinence for the Pharisees to accuse Him of profaning the institution He Himself had established.

Today, the danger in connection with Sabbath observance is not in multiplied restrictions as in the days of the Pharisees, but rather in laxity and neglect of God's holy day, either from forgetfulness of the claims of God, or as a result of believing the lie started by the Pharisees that Jesus really intended to abolish the law.

For both errors, the precept and example of Jesus, who came to "magnify the law, and make it honourable," provide salutary correction and guidance.

If we would discover the true blessing of the Sabbath day we will rest upon it as He, the Carpenter of Nazareth, rested. Like Jesus, it will be our "custom" to join with others in worship and praise of God in His sanctuary. And like Him, too, we will take the opportunity of its sacred hours to do good wherever and whenever occasion affords.

This chapter is based on Mark 3:1-6; Luke 6:6-11; Matthew 12:9-14.

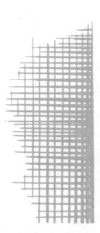

Like Jesus, we should join with others to worship God on the Sabbath day.

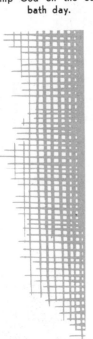

CHAPTER THIRTY-FIVE

Ambassadors of the Kingdom

THE healing of the man with the withered hand on the Sabbath was a turning point of the ministry of Jesus in Galilee, as the healing of the paralytic at Bethesda on the Sabbath had been in His Judean ministry.

After the miracle at Bethesda the religious leaders in Jerusalem made up their minds that Jesus must be silenced and they laid plans to "slay Him."

Following the healing in the Galilean synagogue, the ecclesiastical authorities in the north were "filled with madness," and they too "went forth, and straightway took counsel with the Herodians, how they might destroy Him."

The Pharisees and Herodians had no more in common with each other than had the Pharisees and the Sadducees. But, as representatives of church and state, they were united in their determination to prevent any usurpation of their authority by Jesus. Doubtless the Pharisees hoped to persuade Herod, through his supporters, to arrest Jesus as he had arrested John the Baptist.

By their rejection of the Messiah and Saviour, the rulers of the Jews had now sealed their own rejection as the nation of God's elect. Israel could no longer be used by God as a missionary people to the world. He must lay the foundations of His kingdom in a new spiritual Israel through whom His purpose would be fulfilled. So, not long after His rejection by the leaders in Galilee, Jesus proceeded to organize this new Israel, to define the duties and privileges of citizenship, and to chart its course to ultimate triumph.

This was the reason for the appointment of the twelve apostles at this time as ambassadors of the good tidings.

This was the significance of the Sermon on the Mount, the Magna Charta of the kingdom.

One by one Jesus called His disciples to Him.
By J. J. TISSOT

To prepare for this epochal development in the plan of redemption, Jesus left Capernaum some time in the late summer for the solitude of the hills, where He spent a whole night in earnest communion with God. If men today always followed His example in preparing themselves for God's work, how much more effective their service would be.

The Record states that Jesus went up into "the mountain," indicating a particular height, which must have stood out clearly in the ring of hills surrounding the Plain of Gennesaret. Though its name is not given, there are many who believe that it was the double peak, called the "Horns of Hattin," which rises above the general level of the mountain rim some five miles behind Tiberias. If Jesus followed the coast road to Magdala and then ascended the craggy Valley of Doves He would come out onto the ridge right at its foot. From there He could continue His climb to one of the two horn-like summits. If this was the scene of His all-night vigil, the wide level plain between the two peaks fits very well the description of the place where, the next morning, He spoke to the multitudes.

There are others, however, who would identify the mountain to which Jesus retired with an eminence between eight and nine hundred feet high which lies only about four miles north of Capernaum, not far from the Damascus Road. It also has a level plain at its base and has the merit of being only about half as far from Capernaum as the Horns of Hattin.

Between the two sites it is now quite impossible to decide. This, however, does not in the least matter, for the subsequent events were infinitely more important than the precise spot where they transpired. Well, indeed, has this mountain, wherever it was, been described as the Sinai of the New Testament.

Jesus had doubtless told His disciples where He was going and instructed them to join Him the next morning. Before it was light, therefore, they were up and on their way. As they climbed the slopes of the mountain they saw Jesus coming down toward them, His white robe glistening in the morning sunshine.

Seating Himself upon a convenient rock He looked over the little group and then, with solemn deliberation, called them one by one to Him until twelve disciples were kneeling in a semi-circle at His feet. Then rising, He placed His hands successively upon their heads and "ordained" them to be associates with Him in His sacred ministry.

That Jesus appointed just "twelve" apostles is significant. As the twelve tribes of ancient Israel were descended from Jacob's twelve sons, so the twelve apostles were to be the spiritual progenitors of the "tribes" of the new Israel, whose names will one day grace the foundations of the New Jerusalem.

Of the twelve, Simon, Andrew, John, Philip, and Bartholomew-Nathanael, had confessed themselves His disciples beside the Jordan soon after His baptism and, except when their work demanded their attention, they had been with Him ever since. James, if not with his brother John at the Jordon, must have been introduced to Jesus very soon after His return to Galilee, and Matthew-Levi left his customs post to follow Jesus early in the Capernaum ministry.

Appropriately, therefore, these seven are mentioned first in each of the lists. When the other five—Thomas, James the son of Alphaeus, Judas also called Lebbæus and Thaddeus, Simon the Canaanite or the Zealot, and Judas Iscariot—first joined Jesus we have no record, but they obviously had been intimately associated with Him for some time, or they would not have accompanied the other disciples on their morning journey to meet Jesus.

All had previously been called to discipleship. Now they were ordained as the first of His apostles, or witnesses.

By no human standards would such a strange group have been chosen for so momentous a task. But the Scriptures tell us that Jesus chose "whom He would" and so His choice was perfect—even though He numbered Judas, the betrayer, among the twelve.

Can we discern, as we look at these men, what were the guiding principles in His selection?

We can see immediately whom He did not choose. He did not look for His first disciples among the wealthy, though they might have contributed handsomely to the support of the pioneers of the kingdom. He did not choose any of high social standing, who might have given dignity to the movement. He did not select any from among the learned and cultured in Jewry to gain the respect of the intellectual classes. In due time some of the rich, the distinguished, and the wise, did accept the Gospel, for there is no "respect of persons" with God, but for its first ambassadors He chose "earthen vessels" that the glory of the Gospel might not be in the wisdom of man, but in the power of God.

The disciples Jesus chose were not selected for any social, intellectual, or cultural contribution which they could bring to His cause, but for the completeness of their surrender to Him, their readiness to "leave all"—home, family ties, possessions, prospects—to follow Him, their willingness to be moulded into His likeness, and their preparedness to face anything, privation, hardship, persecution, even martyrdom, to bear the good tidings to men. Such ones, despite their faults and imperfections, He could transform, by His power and grace, into effective witnesses for Him.

The wide variety in the character, temperament, and religious experience of the disciples reveals the appeal of the Gospel and the diversity of talents which God can use in His service. Jesus drew to Himself strong and vigorous men like Simon and James, the thoughtful and reflective like John. He attracted hard-headed men of the world like Matthew and also the shy and diffident like Philip. He conquered the dou'ts of Nathanael-Bartholomew and Thomas. He turned the fanatical patriot Simon Zelotes into a crusader for God. As another great apostle, by inspiration, declared, "The Gospel . . . is the power of God unto salvation to every one that believeth." He is able to save "to the uttermost" all "that come unto God by Him."

The admittance of Judas Iscariot into the company of Christ's disciples might seem surprising, but it was not a mistake. It was permitted as a warning that it is not the "called and chosen," but the "called, and chosen, and faithful" who will enter into the "joy of the Lord."

OPPOSITE

he High Priest of the few
maining Samaritans who still
ve in Nablus, not far from
acob's Well. Beside him is
n ancient copy of the
entateuch which constitutes
e Bible of the Samaritans.

ABOVE

e village of Sychar, where
welt the Samaritan woman
ho talked with Jesus at
Jacob's Well.

RIGHT

peasant woman with her
ater pot in the partly built
urch now enclosing Jacob's
Well.

The plans of Jesus for His chosen band of disciples are comprehended in two simple phrases: "That they should be with Him," and "that He might send them forth."

First, they were to be His disciples. They were to be instructed in the message they were to bear, and to witness the wondrous works which later, by His power, they were to duplicate.

By beholding Him they were to become changed into His likeness. Through His intercession they were to be imbued with His Spirit and power.

Then they would be ready to go forth as His apostles, to share His ministry while He was yet with them, and thereafter to publish the good tidings to earth's far ends in preparation for His return and the establishment of His kingdom of glory.

What a task to commit into the hands of mortal men! No wonder the apostle Paul cried out, in his sense of inadequacy, "Who is sufficient for these things?" and then added in selfless confidence, "Our sufficiency is of God."

While the names of some of these first apostles have been upon the lips of God's

Today the Gospel is being preached throughout the world.

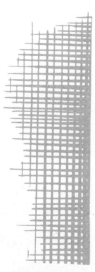

One-time savages and cannibals, like this Solomon Islands chief, are joining in the proclamation of a crucified, risen, and soon-coming Saviour.

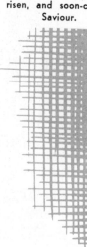

people all down the centuries for the great work of grace accomplished through them, of others we know little or nothing. But they were equally faithful to their task. Though unrecorded by men, their work was not forgotten by God, and it will be rewarded. And so also will the labours of all those other hidden saints down the centuries who have laboured in obscurity, but who will "shine forth" in the kingdom of His glory.

This chapter is based on Mark 3:13-19; Luke 6:12-16.

CHAPTER THIRTY-SIX

The Men
Jesus Chose

FIRST on the list of the apostles in each of the gospels is Simon, whom Jesus surnamed Peter on that fateful morning down by the Jordan. He is placed in this position, and also first among the three most intimate disciples of Jesus —Peter, James, and John—because his warm, ardent, and impulsive nature quickly established him as the leader and spokesman of the little band. This, however, did not confer upon him any primacy of authority, as some have suggested, nor did it indicate any superior wisdom, for Peter had to be rebuked on more than one occasion by Jesus and by his brethren, and only through an act of wondrous grace was he saved from forfeiting for ever his place among the twelve.

Simon's impulsiveness was both his strength and his weakness. He was first at the feet of Jesus after the miraculous draught of fishes on the Sea of Galilee. When Jesus sought an expression of loyalty from His disciples at Cæsarea Philippi, Peter was first to confess his faith. It was Peter who climbed out of the boat on stormy Galilee as Jesus approached across the raging waters, and it was he who instantly drew his knife to protect Jesus from molestation in Gethsemane.

On the other side, however, Peter's precipitancy drew from Jesus a well-merited rebuke when he took it upon himself to dispute with his Master as to what He ought or ought not to do. And, sad to say, Peter was the first of the disciples to deny Jesus on the fatal night of His arrest. It took these bitter experiences to shatter Peter's rash self-confidence and lead him to discover a new strength in God. But when Peter's ardent and generous nature was wholly surrendered to the will of God he was able to take his place in the forefront of the apostolic witness on the day of Pentecost, and became a veritable pillar in the church. With John he was first to suffer bonds and

---

Jesus blesses the little band of disciples whom He had gathered round Him.
By ANTON DORPH

imprisonment for the Gospel. And when his work was done he gladly laid down in martyrdom the life which had been so heroically devoted to Christ.

Is your nature like Peter's before his conversion? Have you so wounded the heart of Jesus by your impulsive waywardness that you feel He can no more have a place for you in His love? Do not despair. If you sincerely repent and cast yourself upon His mercy He can restore you as He did Peter, and direct your energy and enthusiasm for the furtherance of His kingdom.

Next in order among the disciples, and making up with Peter the inner circle of Christ's companions, were the brothers James and John, sons of Zebedee. If their mother was Salome, as many believe, the sister of the virgin Mary, this would make them cousins of our Lord. Zebedee was one of the more prosperous fishermen of Capernaum. Not only had he a good local business, but he also had trade connections in Jerusalem and supplied fish regularly to the house of the high priest. That was how John and Peter were able to go in after Jesus when He was taken there on the night of His betrayal.

James and John shared with · Peter the physical strength necessary for their arduous occupation and they also had in good measure the turbulent, hasty temper of the Galileans. That they merited the surname, "sons of thunder," is shown by their urging Jesus to call down fire upon the Samaritan villagers who refused to give Him shelter.

In other ways, however, they were very different from Peter. Whatever Peter's faults, he was incapable of subterfuge. James and John, however, were not above intriguing with their mother for the chief places of responsibility in the kingdom. Jesus was saddened by their duplicity, but He was as patient with them as He was with Peter. And when they had learned their lesson, the desire for position was completely superseded by a willingness to serve and suffer for the Master.

James, perhaps because he was older than John, undertook no missionary journeys, but for fourteen years after the crucifixion bore a fearless witness to the Gospel in Galilee. His heroic labours were terminated in a martyr death, the first among the apostles, about A.D. 44, at the hands of Herod Agrippa, then tetrarch of Galilee under the Emperor Caligula. Tradition has it that the man who accused James to Herod was converted by his bearing during the trial, and, having asked and received James' forgiveness, was executed with him.

As so often happens with brothers, John and James had their dissimilarities. Beneath his proud and fiery exterior, John had a contemplative nature, which, after he had experienced the purifying effects of divine grace in his heart, transformed him into the "beloved disciple" who "leaned on Jesus' breast." In John, divine love perfected a wondrous union of strength and grace which found full expression in his long ministry and in the inspired writings which he penned.

His loving spirit shines from the pages of his letters to the church, while, through the visions granted to him on Patmos, he thundered the warnings of divine judgment upon the workers of iniquity.

His bold witness to the Gospel, as with the other apostles, made him a target for persecution, and he was banished for a time to Patmos in the reign of the Emperor Diocletian. Under the milder rule of Emperor Nerva, however, he was allowed to return to his ministry among the churches of Asia Minor. There he lived and served longest of all the apostles and was the only one to die a natural death.

In his old age he wrote the last of the New Testament writings, the fourth gospel, which sounded the profoundest depths of the mystery of redemption. Thus, in Jesus' choice of the inner circle of His companions, He showed that the church needs both its heralds and its seers.

Andrew was one of the first two disciples to join Jesus at the prompting of John the Baptist. But while his companion John and his brother Simon became the closest friends of Jesus, Andrew himself never entered that most intimate circle. A lesser man might have been envious and resentful of Jesus' choice. It is surely a testimony to his unselfish nature that he was willing quietly to serve in the place which Jesus allotted to him.

Andrew was not a great evangelist like Peter, nor a great seer like John, but he was one of those kindly souls to whom one instinctively goes with one's problems. That was why, when the Grecian proselytes contacted Philip at the feast in Jerusalem and asked to be taken to Jesus, he sought out Andrew for his advice.

Oh, how much the church stands in need of Andrews who, in their quiet, unassuming way, carry on their ministry of helpfulness, seeking no recognition for themselves and finding their highest joy in seeing souls they have brought to Jesus develop into mighty workers for God.

In harmony with the unselfish nature of Andrew is the tradition that he chose one of the remotest and most uncongenial of mission fields, the barbarian tribes of Scythia, whom he evangelized until his martyrdom. Before the Byzantines, he laid the foundations of the church in Russia.

Philip was the remaining fisherman of the apostolic company. His home was in Bethsaida of Galilee, just south of Capernaum. The fact that he did not seek Jesus out, but was found by Him, suggests that he was slow to recognize Jesus as the Messiah. But when conviction came to him he became an earnest follower of Jesus and a winner of souls. He always found the apprehension of the profound truths of redemption difficult, but he was happy to busy himself with provisioning Jesus and His company. When he saw the five thousand in the wilderness he immediately began to think out how much bread it would take to feed them rather than of the opportunity Jesus had to exercise His wonder-working powers. Later Jesus had to chide Philip for failing to recognize a revelation of the Father in Him.

Yet for all his slowness of mind and weakness of faith Jesus loved Philip's simple devotion, and while He used Philip's practical gifts, he sought to lead him to higher levels of spiritual perception and trust.

That Philip did wonderfully grow in grace and knowledge is evident in the tradition that when the church was scattered by persecution he performed exploits of missionary service in Asia and died at last a martyr for Christ at Hierapolis, in Phrygia.

If Jesus did not despise Philip's one talent, He will certainly not despise ours.

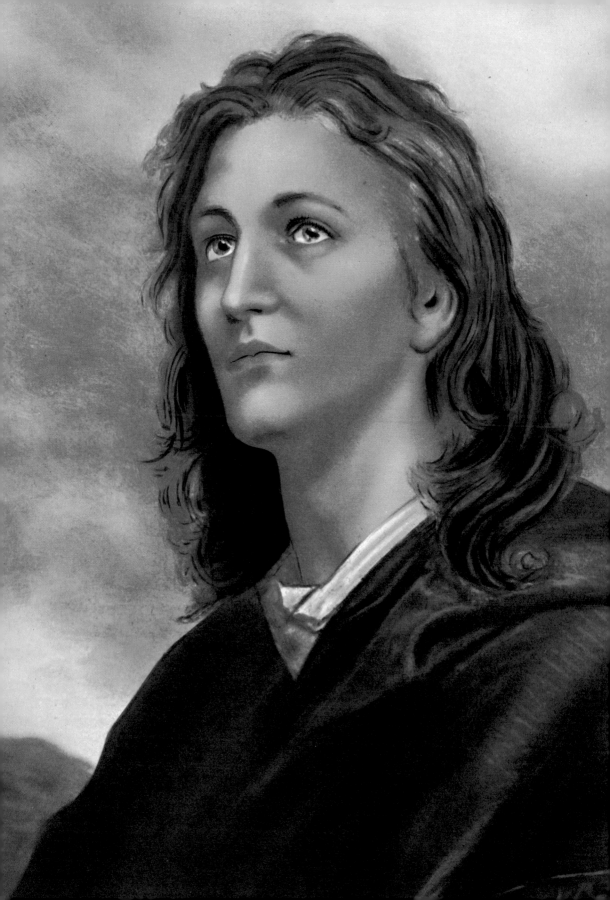

If we will dedicate it to Him, He will multiply it to two, and perhaps even five, for His glory.

Among the disciples there was not only a diffident Philip, but a doubting Thomas. There is no question of his devotion to Jesus, for he was the one who bravely urged his fellow disciples in a time of danger to follow Jesus to Jerusalem, and if necessary to die with Him. But, like Philip, he seemed only able to believe in what was tangible to him. Blessed with but little spiritual insight, he found it difficult to "see the invisible." When, therefore, he was told by the other disciples that Jesus had risen from the dead, he refused to believe until he had seen for himself.

Yet he was an honest doubter and as such Jesus was ready to lead him step by step from doubt to belief. How Thomas must have treasured his memory of the patience of Jesus and of the profound experience which banished his every doubt.

In our day there are many who are "willingly ignorant" of all the evidence of God's activity in the affairs of men. For such He can do nothing, but with the modern Thomases, the honest doubters, He patiently labours until, like the doubting disciple, they too make the confession, "My Lord and my God."

Tradition says that Thomas laboured in Parthia and Persia and perhaps even as far as India and China. There is, indeed, a Mar Thoma church in India today, and St. Thomas' Mountain, near Madras, is claimed as the scene of his martyrdom.

If any disciple more than another revealed what Jesus can do for a man it was Matthew. Previous to meeting Jesus he made no profession of religion, for his occupation shut him out of the synagogue, and his treatment at the hands of the religious leaders had destroyed any vestige of desire for spiritual things. Spurned by his fellow countrymen and bullied by the Roman overlords, his one concern had been to make a fortune and then retire on the fruits of his ill-gotten gains. He was what the Old Testament calls a "profane" man.

But when he first listened to Jesus, Matthew realized that He was different from the priests and rabbis. The more he heard the more he was drawn to this powerful yet kindly Teacher, and before long, he was ready to cast away all his profits and prospects to follow wherever Jesus should lead.

Had Jesus a place for the talents of a converted Matthew? He certainly had, for his literary abilities led to his choice as the inspired penman of one of the gospels.

Matthew's sphere of missionary service, according to one tradition, was Ethiopia. Another mentions the Black Sea region as the field of his labours and he, too, died a martyr's death.

Of the activities of the other disciples, excepting Judas Iscariot, the Scriptures provide little information and only the vaguest traditions have come down to us of their service in the cause of Christ.

Nathanael or Bartholomew of Cana is said to have carried the Gospel as far as

---

John, of all the disciples, best knew and loved his Master.
By J. M. H. HOFFMAN

India. Later, he laboured in Southern Europe and was eventually flayed alive and crucified like his Master in Albania.

James, the son of Alphæus, was probably not a brother of Matthew, although Mark gives Alphæus as the name also of Matthew's father. If they had been brothers, their names would certainly have been associated like Peter and Andrew, James and John. James the Less, as he is sometimes called, seems to have stayed in and around Jerusalem to strengthen the church there and, in such close proximity to the rulers of the Jews, he quickly became an object of jealousy and hatred. Eventually, it is said, they laid violent hands upon him, dragging him up to the pinnacle of the temple, and hurling him down into the court below. Mangled and dying he managed to get onto his knees and pray for his murderers. Showers of stones then put an end to his sufferings and his brains were beaten out with a fuller's club.

Judas, not Iscariot, was the son of an unidentified man named James. He is named Lebbæus in Matthew's gospel and Thaddeus by Mark. If these names were surnames given by Jesus to sum up his character he was a "hearty" man and an "encourager" of his brethren. Tradition has it that he laboured for the Gospel in Persia and witnessed his last confession in a martyr's death.

The second Simon in the disciple group is called Simon the Canaanite by Matthew and Mark, indicating that he came from Cana of Galilee. One may well wonder whether he first saw Jesus at the wedding in Cana and whether Nathanael had a part in bringing him to the Saviour.

Luke calls him Simon Zelotes. This suggests that before he came to Jesus he belonged to the patriotic underground movement founded by Judas of Gamala, whose members had sworn their enmity to the Romans and would stop at nothing to drive them from the land. Their heroes were the Maccabeans who for a period before Christ actually re-established Jewish independence.

What courage Jesus had to bring together into the ranks of the disciples a proud zealot like Simon, who hated the Romans with every fibre of his patriotic being, and a taxgatherer like Matthew, who had actually sold himself to the Romans for gain! And what a miracle of grace it was that transformed their hearts and made them brethren and co-labourers in the cause of Christ.

Simon is believed to have laboured in Egypt and North Africa. Some say he came to Britain, and that he also suffered martyrdom.

The zeal and service of these lesser known disciples are unrecorded in sacred Writ and their traditions are vague in the annals of the church, but they are remembered by God and their names will shine out from the foundations of the New Jerusalem.

Last and strangest of all the characters who found a place among the disciples was Judas Iscariot, so named because he came from Kerioth, a little Judean town commonly identified with el Karjetein, south of Hebron. He was thus the only Judean among the disciples.

Seeing that Jesus saw "from the beginning" the evil traits hidden beneath the smooth profession of this cultured and capable man, and that He knew he would turn traitor, why did Jesus, when he offered himself, admit him into the ranks of the disciples? The reason was because the experience of Judas was to be a terrible lesson to the church.

Judas believed that Jesus was the Messiah and he was ready to devote his life and his energies to the establishment of Christ's kingdom, but he was more interested in the material benefits which he would receive for his services than in its spiritual privileges. One gathers that he came of an influential family and that, in accepting the control of the common fund, he already pictured himself as Jesus' chief executive. His dishonesty in administering it, however, shows that he completely failed to understand the difference between service in Christ's kingdom and in the world.

When Jesus refused to be made an earthly king and began to warn His disciples that He was destined to suffer and to die, Judas was bitterly disappointed, and to compel Jesus to assert Himself he determined to procure His arrest. Little did he realize, however, that by this treacherous act he was giving Jesus up to His death.

Judas was allowed to play out his part to its bitter end without exposure, just as Satan was allowed to remain beside the throne of God till his rebellion came into the open, as a warning that the most sacred office is no guarantee against apostasy. On a later occasion Jesus declared that in the judgment many would protest that they had "prophesied" in His name and in His name "done many wonderful works," yet Jesus would be compelled to say to them, "I never knew you." Like Judas they may succeed in deceiving their fellow Christians, but their hearts are naked and open to Him with whom we have to do, and their hypocrisy will ultimately be exposed.

The career of Judas underlines the warning penned by the apostle Paul, "Examine yourselves, whether ye be in the faith." For only such will stand in the pure light of the judgment of God.

In his terrible fall Judas provided an unintentional yet powerful testimony to the character of Christ, for as a spy among the disciples he could certainly have provided evidence against Christ if there had been any.

But though he betrayed Jesus, He had not a word of accusation against Him, and in his bitter remorse he confessed to the Jewish rulers that he had betrayed "innocent" blood.

Here then we have the men whom Jesus chose to be His ambassadors to the world. Beneath their many faults and imperfections, He saw in each, even Judas, qualities and talents which He could use in the proclamation of the Good Tidings. Patiently He uncovered the traits which marred their capacity for service, and as, all except Judas, they submitted to His discipline and yielded to His power, they were miraculously transformed into vessels meet for His use.

And just as surely as Jesus had a place in His service for Peter, James, and John and the rest of the disciples, He has a place for us if we will let Him cleanse our hearts and make us into what He wants us to be for Him.

This chapter is based on Mark 3:13-19; Luke 6:12-16.

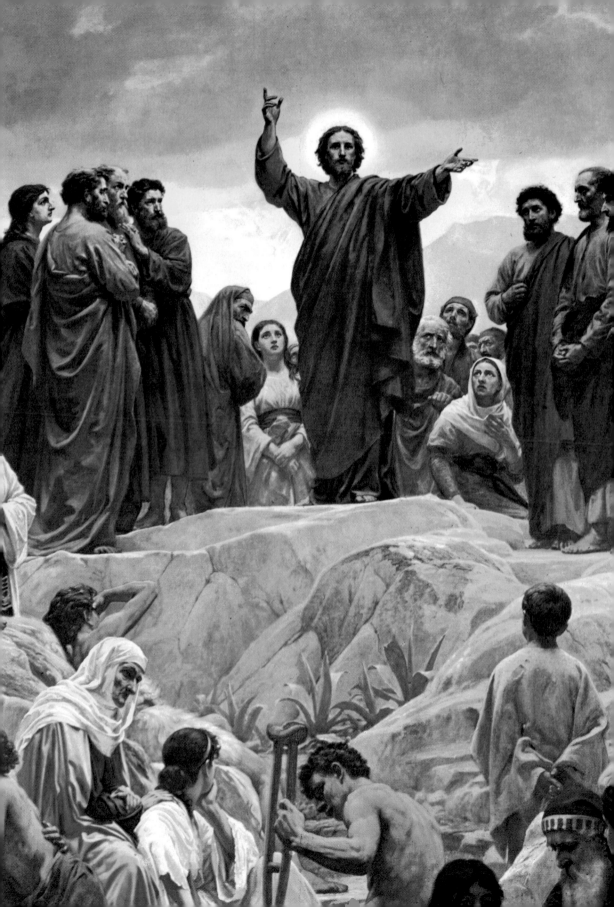

On the Mount of Blessing

WHEN Jesus came down with His disciples from the mountain of the ordination it was not long before a great crowd gathered around Him by the seaside.

Among them were townspeople from Capernaum and countryfolk from the villages scattered over the Plain of Gennesaret. There were many, too, from as far away as Jerusalem and Judea in the south, and from the region of Tyre and Sidon in the north. Hearing of the wonderful works which Jesus had done in Galilee, they brought along their sick ones to receive His healing touch. And they were not disappointed, for "there went virtue out of Him and He healed them all."

So great was the concourse of people who came for healing and to hear His teaching that the narrow beach was soon too confined for all to get near. When, therefore, He had finished His healing ministry Jesus retired again to the hills, followed by His disciples and the multitude. Selecting a prominent rock on the grassy slope where He could be seen and heard by all, He sat down, after the manner of the teachers of that day, and began the discourse which has ever since been known as the "Sermon on the Mount."

It may be wondered why Jesus chose to deliver so considerable a body of teaching at this time, and to this particular congregation, but when we think of the events which preceded it we can understand the reason.

The rejection of Jesus by the religious leaders in Judea and Galilee convinced Him that the time had come to inaugurate the new Israel, the church, to take the place of fleshly Israel. Early that morning, therefore, after a night of earnest prayer, Jesus had appointed the twelve disciples as representatives of the "tribes" of the new Israel. Now He was to proclaim the constitution and laws of the kingdom and outline the spiritual qualifications of those who were to be its subjects.

In His "Sermon on the Mount" Jesus explained the way of "blessing" in this life and the qualifications for an inheritance in the eternal home.   By H. OLRIK

That this great pronouncement was made neither in a synagogue nor in the temple, but from a mountain pulpit under the blue heavens, underlines the new spiritual order He was initiating. It was from Mount Sinai that God gave to ancient Israel their commission as His missionary people. Now, upon another mountain, Jesus founded the church which was to carry the Gospel invitation to the ends of the earth.

"The Beatitudes," with which Jesus began His discourse, vividly outline the way of "blessedness" in this life and the qualifications for citizenship in the eternal home of the "blessed." And like God's standard of righteousness proclaimed on Sinai, it begins with man's relation to God and then goes on to delineate his relations with his fellow men.

"Blessed are the poor in spirit," began Jesus, "for theirs is the kingdom of heaven." There was good reason for Jesus putting this qualification first, for it was precisely on this point that the Jews had failed. Like the highly-placed Lucifer in the heavenly courts, they had become exalted by the divine choice and had forgotten the pit whence they were dug. As Paul later described them, "Behold, thou art called a Jew, and restest in the law, and makest thy boast of God, and . . . art confident that thou thyself art a guide of the blind, a light of them which are in darkness." Their estimate of themselves was typified by the Pharisee's prayer in the temple, "God, I thank Thee, that I am not as other men."

But just as spiritual pride brought about the downfall of Lucifer, it forfeited for Israel their place in the redemptive purpose of God. So now, as Jesus began the work of gathering anew the subjects of His kingdom, He made it clear that those only would qualify who were conscious of their sinfulness and who felt their need of divine forgiveness and mercy. Only to those who admit their spiritual poverty does Jesus offer the riches of His grace. Only such does He invite to become "partakers of the inheritance of the saints."

Enumerating the second of the marks of the true children of God, Jesus went on, "Blessed are they that mourn; for they shall be comforted." Those who are "poor in spirit," and are conscious of how far short they fall of the glory of God, will sincerely sorrow for the sin that has separated them from Him. To them comes the assurance of God's comfort. True repentance evokes His mercy and forgiveness, and the sorrow of the sinner is turned to joy in His salvation.

Those, on the other hand, who delight in sin and laugh at God's judgments will one day have their foolish laughter turned to "weeping and gnashing of teeth." How much better is it then to mourn our sins now with godly sorrow and receive the comfort of God, than to wait until the day of recompense when there will be judgment, not comfort, for those who mourn too late.

Upon those who, in deep poverty of spirit and sorrow for sin, come to Him, Jesus pronounces His third "beatitude." "Blessed are the meek: for they shall inherit the earth." Meekness is often regarded as synonymous with gentleness, but the word which Jesus used really means "teachableness." Those who, in the pride of their own wisdom, persist in going their own way, will discover too late that it leads to death and destruction. But if, like little children, we sit at His feet and learn of Him, He will direct our steps into the way of life. Seeking a wisdom not of God, our first parents were driven from Eden. To the meek, the lost inheritance will be restored.

To complete the picture of the redemptive process portrayed in the first three beatitudes, Jesus added the fourth, "Blessed are they which do hunger and thirst after righteousness: for they shall be filled."

When we come to Christ in repentance and faith our lives are cleansed or emptied of unrighteousness, and a hunger and a thirst for God's righteousness is born in us. In response to that hunger and thirst, Jesus declares, "I am the Bread of life: he that cometh to Me shall never hunger; and he that believeth on Me shall never thirst." His Word becomes our daily bread. His Spirit is as a well of water springing up into everlasting life. "In Him," adds the apostle Paul, "ye are made full."

Marvellous indeed is the saving grace which can restore fallen man, so marred by sin, to the "measure of the stature of the fullness of Christ." As the people listened to this wonderful outline of the plan of redemption they could not but contrast it with the teaching of the proud Pharisees and the worldly Sadducees, and many that day determined to follow Jesus and seek the character which would fit them for a place in His kingdom.

The last six commandments of the Decalogue set forth the human relationships born of a true relationship to God, and in like manner the remaining four beatitudes show the outworking of grace in the life of the child of God.

Because he has himself received "mercy," he will be "merciful" toward his fellows, forgiving those who do him wrong because God, for Christ's sake, has forgiven him. He will recognize in others what he was before he came to Christ, and in his heart there will be, not condemnation, but an earnest desire to lead them to the Source of pardon and peace.

From a "pure heart" will spring that purity of life, so different from the ceremonial cleanness of the Pharisees. This entitles men to "see" God now by faith and one day to see Him face to face in His kingdom.

The followers of Him who came to bring "on earth peace, good will toward men," will themselves be "peacemakers," seeking to reconcile men to God. Their lives will be oases of peace in a world of sin and strife.

Like their Master, who was "oppressed" and "afflicted" without complaint, they will rejoice when men revile and persecute them and "say all manner of evil" against them falsely, knowing that their witness, like that of the prophets and Jesus before them, will bear fruit for the kingdom of God, and that the light afflictions of this present life will be swallowed up in an eternal reward.

What a picture Jesus drew of the character of the children of God! No wonder He declared significantly of them that they would be the "salt of the earth," the "light of the world," and a "city set on a hill."

The salt found among the rocks around the Dead Sea was prized as a savour or seasoning, as well as being the most effective preservative available in the days before refrigerators and cold storage. God's purpose for the Jews was that they should be the spiritual "salt" which would preserve all nations with the savour of righteousness.

OPPOSITE

A street in Jerusalem.

ABOVE

The Dome of the Rock, which stands upon the site of the ancient temple in Jerusalem.

RIGHT

The Mount of Olives seen through the arches surround- the Dome of the Rock.

By their own folly, however, they lost the divine savour and had become fit only to be "cast out, and to be trodden under foot." In their place Jesus was now calling forth a new people, His church, who would reflect His character and spread their holy savour in the lives of all men everywhere.

That is what the Gospel has done all down the ages. Not only has it delivered multitudes from the corruption of sin, but it has actually saved degraded tribes of mankind from physical extinction. Truly Christians and Christian communities have been the "salt" of the earth, and but for the restraints which they have placed upon human society, civilization might ere this have perished.

In His second illustration Jesus compared His people to the little Eastern lamps which were the usual means of illumination in that day. When darkness fell these lamps, consisting of a wick floating in a bowl of oil, were lighted and placed upon candlesticks or in niches in the wall from which they illuminated every corner of the humble dwellings.

Had the Jews fulfilled God's intention, they would have been "the light of the world," but they hid the gift of God under the bushel of their own pride and self-sufficiency so long that it was snuffed out, leaving them to stumble along as blind men in the darkness.

Jesus came to kindle a new light in the lives of those who received Him that the glory of God might be shed abroad to the ends of the earth.

The third illustration Jesus used was especially apt in Palestine where cities were set for safety upon the hilltops rather than down in the open valleys. From where Jesus spoke the people could see the white houses of more than one such city gleaming in the morning sun. Just like that the church was to be, witnessing to the Gospel of grace and offering men a divine refuge from the assaults of Satan, man's direst foe.

"Blessed" indeed was the call of Jesus to the multitudes on

On Mount Sinai God declared His law, and on another mountain in Galilee Jesus set forth the "way of blessedness" for all who would receive Him.

By DUBUFE

the mount and blessed is the life to which He is still calling men and women, boys and girls, today. Glorious, too, is the "home of the blessed" in which He is reserving a place for all His children hereafter. That life and that home can be yours if you will cast away your pride and self-sufficiency, if you will recognize yourself as a sinner standing in need of the grace of God, if you will let Him empty your life of sin and fill it with His righteousness and peace.

This chapter is based on Matthew 5:1-16; Luke 6:20-26.

NORTHERN PALESTINE
in
BIBLE TIMES

SYROPHOENICIA

GALILEE

● TYRE

● ACCHO, PTOLEMAIS

CA

MAC

Mt. Carmel

● CANA

NAZARETH T

Plain of Esdraelon

● NAIN

Mt.

● SHUNEM

● MEGIDDO

Mt. Gilboa

● JEZREEL

BETH

● CAESAREA